Career Coach

A step-by-step guide to help your teen
find their life's purpose

DEARBHLA KELLY

D1076792

Gill & Macmillan
Hume Avenue
Park West
Dublin 12
www.gillmacmillanbooks.ie

© Dearbhla Kelly 2015

978 07171 6855 2

Design and print origination by O'K Graphic Design, Dublin
Edited by Jane Rogers
Printed and bound by GraphyCems, Spain

This book is typeset in 11/15 pt Adobe Garamond.

The paper used in this book comes from the wood pulp of managed
forests. For every tree felled, at least one tree is planted, thereby
renewing natural resources.

A CIP catalogue record for this book is available from the British
Library.

ACKNOWLEDGEMENTS

I would like to thank all the people who supported me on the journey in writing this book. First, thanks to my mentor Nick Williams; to Rachael Kilgallon of 'The Career Hub' for all her valuable input; to Alan Richardson for his inspiration; to Muireann Ni Dhuigneain for her coaching; to Patricia Mc Geever for her hospitality; to Liam Harkin, guidance counsellor, and Kathleen Brennan, former guidance inspector, who lent me their thoughts in the initial stages; and to Cróna Gallagher, adult education officer, who granted me a two-year career break from Donegal Education and Training Board (ETB). In particular, thanks to Marian Byrne, parent coach, who offered great parenting advice for this book.

Thanks to all the people who took part in the interviews and case studies. They shine a light on the value of following your passion and the value of having the right attitude. Thanks especially to the parents of the students of Abbey Vocational School and Errigal College in Donegal ETB who took part in a pilot project based on career coaching elements of this book. This book has been inspired by all the students and colleagues I have worked with in schools: Castleblayney College, Ballybay Community College and Gaelscoil Coláiste Mhuire, Cabra, St Mary's Baldoyle, Careers Advisory Service, Trinity College Dublin, and Adult Education Services, Donegal ETB.

A special thanks to my parents, Roisin and Donal, and my family and friends, who have cheered me on. Last but not least, thanks to Gill & Macmillan for publishing this book.

About the author

Dearbhla Kelly has been in education training and guidance since 1991. She has been working as a Guidance Counsellor in secondary schools with Cavan and Monaghan ETB, in adult guidance with Donegal ETB and as a careers advisor in Trinity College Dublin. She uses a mixture of life coaching, NLP techniques, careers advice and counselling in order to give people practical solutions to finding their purpose and following their career dreams.

Dearbhla loves to walk and has roamed the Camino, completed in the Paris Marathon and strolled the streets of Japan, where she lived for 8 years. Dearbhla now lives in Letterkenny, Co. Donegal.

Praise for Dearbhla Kelly's work

Career Coach really opened up my mind to the fact that career guidance and preparation starts long before the leaving certificate cycle. It gave me a wonderful insight into confidence building techniques and communication methods and the rewards of using them is starting to show! I now have clear paths for both of my daughters. Together we were able to discover the best career fit. I would highly recommend that the tools in *Career Coach* should be mandatory for all parents of second-level children.

MARY BRADLEY
(Mary Bradley participated in a pilot career coaching programme delivered
by Dearbhla Kelly for parents of the students of the Abbey Vocational School
and Errigal College, Donegal ETB)

Ryan was in Leaving Cert year with no idea what to study at college. I arranged a meeting with Dearbhla for career guidance. After that meeting his mind was made up. He knew exactly what direction he was going to take. Six months into the course, there are no regrets; there is no going back, only forward.

VERA HAUGHEY

My son opened up for the first time to Dearbhla about what he wanted to do. He tends to be shy and until then his dreams were locked up inside. Dearbhla's approach helped him express himself and his dreams in music production. Afterwards, he felt more confident and able to follow through with his goals.

TERESA ROPER

Contents

CONTENTS

Foreword

I remember being excited about the pending careers advice session at Hornchurch Grammar School. It was 1973 and I was 15. I sensed there must be a wonderful world of work opportunities and experiences available to me and my fellow students. I was looking forward to having a world of possibilities opened up to me.

I should have been suspicious. The session was going to be run by our physics teacher, Mr Jones. He seemed to be in his twenties, and had probably gone straight from studying to teaching. I had heard that he was newly married and needed to earn some more money by taking on the careers advice role too.

The session went something like this: 'Any questions? There are brochures here on careers in teaching and accounting.' That was it! I left feeling less inspired than before I went in, but anxious now too, because everyone else seemed to know what they wanted to do.

My parents weren't much help either. They said I could do whatever I liked and whatever I wanted to. But that was the problem – I didn't know what I wanted to do! I wanted someone to inspire me, and open up the world to me. To get me excited, to ask me questions like, 'What do you feel you were born to do?' 'What would inspire you?' 'What would fulfil you?' 'What is in your heart that wants to be expressed?' 'What do you love deeply?' 'What can't you stop doing?'

But no one ever did ask me those questions. Luckily, I did begin to ask myself those questions over a decade later and eventually found what I was born to do, what truly inspires me and fulfils me. I wish there had been a Dearbhla around in 1973 for me, my parents and at my school, and I would have got there much quicker.

I first met Dearbhla in a conference room in Croke Park in Dublin in 2008, and we have been in touch ever since. I was immediately struck by two things: the twinkle in her eye and how much she cared about young people and helping them make inspired and empowered career choices.

I sensed an ambition born of inspiration and of a deep desire to contribute rather than a need for self-aggrandisement. She was a woman on a mission. I have seen Dearbhla stay committed in the long run, build and nurture relationships, seize opportunities when they arose and create opportunities when they didn't exist before.

This book is one of the many fruits of that perseverance and long-term commitment. She cares deeply about us being happy in our work and that we get to express the best of ourselves in what we do for a living.

Dearbhla understands the power and influence that family and friends have on teenagers' career choices and decisions, even when those people don't realise the power they have. Dearbhla helps you realise that you do have a positive impact and shows how to use your influence to open hearts and minds, to open up possibilities to discover, and to nurture dreams. She knows that opportunity is an inside job, and whatever is going on in the economy, there are always tremendous possibilities and great hope. She makes the whole process of becoming a coach to teenagers understandable and doable. She believes in the resourcefulness of everyone. She knows that the desire to support and help needs to be matched with the skills of coaching, listening and validation in order to be effective. This book delivers those skills richly and abundantly.

Thank you, Dearbhla, for writing this book. So many lives are already richer because of you and your work and the gift of this book means that so many more lives will be enhanced too.

Nick Williams, London, March 2015
Author of nine books, including *The Work We Were Born To Do*,
and founder of the Spiritual Pro Global Community
www.iamnickwilliams.com

Introduction

❧

The Golden Eagle

A man found an eagle's egg and placed it under a brooding hen. The eaglet hatched with the chickens and grew to be like them. He clucked and cackled, scratched the earth for worms, flapped his wings and managed to fly a few feet in the air.

Years passed. One day, the eagle, now grown old, saw a magnificent bird before him in the sky. It glided gracefully and majestically against the powerful wind with scarcely a movement of its golden wings. Spellbound, the eagle asked, 'Who is that?'

'That is the king of the birds', said his neighbour. 'He belongs to the sky. We belong to the earth – we're chickens.'

So the eagle lived and died a chicken for that's what he thought he was.

ANTHONY DE MELLO, THE SONG OF THE BIRD

Your Role as Career Coach

Nowadays, due to the change in the economic climate, we are looking at a complete shift in the world of work. When people of my generation were growing up, lifetime employment and permanent pensionable posts were plentiful and offered guarantees. Today our young people are moving into a period of contractual work, less certainty, and a need for self-promotion and expertise. In short, they need to be their own leaders and manage their own careers.

In a recent survey of children in the UK, 92 per cent of the children polled said that parents were among their most important influences. Only five per cent would not consult their parents when making career decisions. (Source: GTI Media Research, *Parental Influence on Children's Academic and Employment Choices* (2014).)

Because you have such a significant role to play in your teenager fulfilling their potential, it makes sense to be informed of practical ways to help your child take steps now towards a successful future. There are no shortcuts to discovering 'the work you were born to do'. Helping your teen discover their calling or vocation in life requires many conversations and these conversations aren't always straightforward. One day your teen wants to study medicine and the next she wants to be a deep sea diver! Teenagers' career preferences can change according to what their friends are talking about doing, what colleges their friends are choosing, etc. This toing and froing can be a huge worry for parents and the process can last several years. This book will help you as a parent to engage fully with your teen in the present and show you ways to prepare together for whatever the future holds. Please keep in mind throughout this book that there are in schools professional guidance counsellors who are qualified sources of information on career choices. They are available to help your teen and may provide information evenings for parents on matters such as subject choice and the CAO. Encourage your teen to make an appointment and make use of this vital professional service. Guidance counsellors can also support students who have issues or concerns that are affecting their participation in school. If guidance is not available in your teen's school, you might find it useful to consult a private practitioner; a list is supplied on the Institute of Guidance Counsellors' (IGC) website, www.igc.ie.

This book will give you tools to guide your teen and help them voice their thoughts, opinions, concerns, dreams and excitement about their future. It will be a reference point over three to five years that will help you support and direct your teen in choosing a satisfying career. It will teach you practical ways to guide and motivate your teenager and it provides tasks and activities which you can do together. By working together, you can both develop the skills needed to help your child build a joyful career. My wish is that you will encourage your teen to stay true to their talents and to concentrate on the activities that bring them joy and energy – even if it takes them along unconventional routes. Sometimes, your teen may have to take the scenic route to their career and to a 'slow-cooked' success.

By the end of this book you will:

1. Have learned techniques that help **increase confidence** and areas of ability in your teenager

2. Have learned how to **identify abilities, skills, talents, passions and values** in your teenager and how to use them as signposts to their future careers

3. Know how to **motivate and encourage** your teenager towards their future life dreams

4. Learn how to **practically link your teenager's dreams to reality** by getting them to look at the world of work

5. Understand ways to **increase your teenager's chances of future employment** and encourage a mindset/attitude that can adapt to the changing face of the world of work

6. Have learned ways of developing resilience in your teenager that will help them **turn setbacks into opportunities**

7. Know what **career resources** to use that will identify your teenager's personality, learning style and career interests

8. Know how to find ways to **test out the world of work**

9. Help your teenager build their **inner strength in the face of change**

10. Introduce your teenager to the ideas of **abundance and creativity**.

Between each of these steps, thirteen successful people will share their career insights and wisdom in an interview-style format. These are featured as 'My Career' at the end of each step. Some of these interviewees followed traditional academic paths; others took vocational or apprenticeship routes – academia is not for everyone. What shines out from the interviews is that these people stayed true to their interests and they still love what they do. They are committed to their craft or field; they value excellence and display a solid work ethic; they believe in going the extra mile and are good decision-makers; they learn from and model others; and they believe in continuous improvement. It is worth noting that when some of the interviewees were teenagers, they had no clear vision of what they wanted to do, but their careers unfolded as they matured. In addition, it seems that they all attracted success by cultivating the right attitude. As motivational speaker Zig Ziglar said, 'it is your attitude, not your aptitude, that determines your altitude'.

The appendices at the end of the book will provide you with information and websites covering topics such as the Central Applications Office (CAO), points, apprenticeships, year out, PLCs, mature students, access and disability supports. It is hoped that this section will signpost you in the direction of useful information that will help you and your teen.

I will make suggestions throughout the book about ways in which you can increase your teenager's self-esteem by focusing on strengths, developing self-knowledge and creating clear goals and life dreams. If you put some of these suggestions into practice, your teenager will develop positive thinking, assertiveness and communication skills, and they will also start thinking about self-presentation. The aim is to help your teenager become more self-confident in their choices.

By using this book you can help your teen fly high and increase their own range of possibilities.

Who is this Book For?

Whether you are a parent of teenagers starting the secondary school process or preparing to leave it, or you are reading this book out of curiosity and a belief in young people, it will provide you with tools that will inform and excite you about the range of opportunities available to teenagers in opening the door to their future. It is my hope that by engaging in this process in an open way with your child, they will discover 'the work they were born to do' and that work will give them meaning and satisfaction in a way that serves others and makes a difference.

❖

MY CAREER

Robert Chambers
Hairdresser and Business Owner
www.robertchambers.ie

Robert opened the first hairdressing school in Ireland and was the first hairdresser in Ireland to be inaugurated into the Irish Hairdressing Hall of Fame. He has been in operation for forty years and has three salons in Dublin and two hairdressing academies.

> *'Health and happiness before business ... and then business.'*

How did your career in hairdressing begin?

At 16, I went to work as an apprentice fitter/turner with Roadstone. I had come first in Ireland in the equivalent of today's Junior Cert in mechanical drawing and metalwork. In the meantime, my older brother had become a hairdresser and he always seemed happy, he had nice clothes and his own money. I decided that I wanted some of what he had. I asked my Dad to take me to a well-known Dublin salon called Jules to see if they would give me some experience. I stayed there for ten months, but got no practical training until eventually the guy in the perfumery taught me how to use a scissors and I began cutting children's hair. When I was more confident, I asked one of the stylists what was the best salon in Dublin. He said 'the Witches Hut', so I went there, took a look in the window, and what I saw was incredible! I went back the next week and asked for a job, and they gave me one! It continued from there and in the summers I would go to London to train at Vidal Sassoon, watching the stylists working during the days and styling hair models myself in the evenings.

Did you always want to do what you do now?

It never came into my mind. I thought I would end up doing something related to engineering or architecture. I grew up on a farm, so I was used to using my hands; we always had to improvise and come up with solutions and make things. I loved making things. That was an indicator that I was good with technical detail, which is a requirement for precision hairdressing.

What do you enjoy most about what you do now?

The easiest part of my week is cutting hair, which I do two days a week. It comes naturally to me; it doesn't involve making business and financial decisions. I enjoy meeting a new client every hour, mixing with the staff, etc. I think that there is something special about the atmosphere in a hairdressing salon; it's creative, fun, warm and full of interesting and sometimes unusual people.

What is the toughest thing about your job?

The disappointment and frustration when staff let you down and dealing with the financial side of a business. Like all businesses, hairdressing is competitive and you have to constantly re-invest money back into it, especially if you are at the top end. Interior design constantly needs to be updated and money is needed to do that, even in tough economic times.

What motivates you?

I think that I'm just a positive person in general. As soon as a problem arises, I don't dwell on the problem, I come up with possible solutions. Being positive is also more enjoyable than being negative. I look at the good points: I'm not hungry or cold and I've a great wife and children.

Who or what inspired you along the way?

Tony Rogers (my boss in the Witches Hut); Vidal Sassoon; fashion and the visual side of hairdressing. It was an electrifying time when I started out in the 1960s. It was exploding with excitement, fashion, music and freedom.

What advice on getting started would you give young people who want a career in the same field?

You can go the apprentice route or train in a private academy, where you will have the chance to make money sooner. You get what you put into it; you can come out as a good hairdresser or an amazing hairdresser. It depends on your determination. Prepare a very good CV, make a list of select salons, visit those salons, and ask for a thirty-second meeting with the owner/manager. I'm a great believer in making a visual impression. Always keep in mind that you continually need to work with people better than you to grow your skills and maintain your standards.

What has been the biggest lesson in your career to date?

Professionals can give you advice, but it is not written in stone and you still have to work through things yourself and apply your intelligence. You are walking the plank alone when you run your own business. Try to keep your ego in check and keep a level head.

If you had a motto what would it be?

Health and happiness before business ... and then business.

Without health you have nothing. Business is not the beginning or the end of everything.

What advice would you give your 16-year-old self?
I've no regrets, I've had an interesting, exciting time so far – the people, the travel, the work. I'd do the same again. Two of my children are in the industry, so I see that as a stamp of approval that I did the right thing.

Maybe I'd say 'read more'. But don't believe everything you read: take it on board, but make your own decisions, develop the capacity to think independently, read for the benefit of what others say, but reach your own conclusions.

❖

What is Coaching?

~

The premise of this book is that you as a parent can act as a coach to your child. First, however, **what exactly is 'coaching'**? Here's an explanation from parent coach and mother of three teenagers, Marian Byrne:

> Coaching is a collaborative relationship and process which helps the client (in this case your teenager) to set and work towards their goals and aspirations. It works on the basis that they are the experts on themselves. At this point, I know that your parental instincts are screaming, 'My teenager is not a life expert!' Bear with me, though.

According to Marian, 'At a very basic level, coaching is listening and asking questions.' Coaching aims to help the person to reach their potential by:

- Helping them identify and develop positive ways of thinking and acting rather than imposing a set way of being or doing on them
- Reflecting what the person says back to them rather than directing them
- Helping them identify their strengths
- Highlighting what areas may need extra focus and attention so that the person can achieve their goals
- Encouraging, supporting and challenging as appropriate, while always remaining non-judgemental.

Marian says:

> As parents, we will naturally be able to do some (and well done
> if you can do all) of the above. We may find it easy to challenge
> them and help them push the boundaries of their comfort
> zones to achieve; yet, we may be less comfortable championing
> them when they have fallen short in some way. We may be able
> to see what they can do better, yet forget to give them detailed
> praise and feedback in relation to their strengths.

You will find tried and tested tips and techniques on communicating
with your teen throughout this book. So, before you begin career
coaching your teen, Step 1 will look at some ways in which you as
a parent can improve communication with your teenager.

❖

MY CAREER

Diarmuid Gavin
Garden Designer

Ireland's acclaimed garden designer has brought garden designs
to new, distinct levels. Winner of the RDS Gold Award in 1991
and 1993, Diarmuid also won gold at Chelsea for 'The Irish
Sky Garden' in 2011. He is a well-known presenter of gardening
programmes on BBC and RTÉ.

'My biggest lesson has been not to give up, to follow a dream.'

How did your career in gardening/horticulture begin?

When I left school I felt that I'd love to be a gardener or a chef. My first job application that was accepted was for a commis chef in a restaurant. I loved that and stayed for four months. I had applied for another position at the same time – in a plant shop in Dublin city centre – and it was subsequently offered to me. I changed without hesitation as I had realised that I definitely wanted to create gardens. After three years there in Mackeys of Mary Street, I left to study in the Botanic Gardens in Glasnevin. Immediately after graduation, I set up my own business, designing and building gardens for clients.

Did you always want to do what you do now?

I think the teenage years can be very confusing. When considering career choices, there's an inordinate amount of pressure from schools and families to make decisions that could determine and shape a life. I knew I wanted to do something creative. When I was young, I wanted to make stuff. This could have meant anything from being an artist, a potter or a chef. I felt that there was opportunity in gardening, not because I loved the gardens I saw, but because I didn't and I felt I could change them.

What do you enjoy most about what you do now?

I've an extremely varied working life, one that is never constant and often packed with surprises. I most love working with a team to create gardens. The design process is a fairly solitary one, but when it comes to implementation you are surrounded by people and you work with them to achieve a common goal. I love to work with soil and plants and in different places. It's extraordinarily fulfilling to completely change a piece of land, to give it a new identity, to add some interest, mystery, colour and fun. But I also love communicating about gardens, writing, making television programmes and lecturing. The best thing about these is the preparation: pushing yourself to explore other people's ideas, gain an understanding of them and relaying those lessons to an audience.

What's the toughest thing about your job?

There aren't too many tough aspects to my job as I am in a position where I get lots of opportunities and I get to work with fantastic people. However, if I were a 'jobbing' garden designer, it could be tough. Clients sometimes don't value the skills associated with planning a garden and often, garden designers and landscape architects can find it difficult to get paid properly for their work. The hours can be very long and sometimes it's not so much fun to be outdoors in the long, cold, often wet winter months.

What motivates you?

I'm motivated first by what always motivated me, the excitement of creating gardens. I can't imagine feeling the same sense of satisfaction in any other role. Making the most of the opportunities that I have been given also motivates me. I never expected to have a voice, to get the opportunity to be listened to and to get involved in situations outside of my skill set (e.g. reality shows in the North Pole, learning to dance, etc.). So living up to the possibilities that life presents is a great motivator.

Who or what inspired you along the way?

I've been inspired by things that people have said to me and the achievements of others ... garden designers such as Roberto Burle Marx, Percy Thrower, the architecture of Le Corbusier and Frank Lloyd Wright, and movies such as *Charlie and the Chocolate Factory*.

What advice on getting started would you give to young people who want a career in the same field?

Nothing comes easily. The gardening industry is a tough one but it's a passionate one. There's a danger that people see gardeners on television achieving a degree of fame or fortune and believe those results are something to aspire to. If you love gardening and are imagining a career in it, show what you can do. Demonstrate your abilities either at home, in friends' gardens, through gardening clubs in school or by seeking work in garden centres or with landscape contractors during the holiday periods. If nobody will give you a paid role, offer to work for free. Put everything into it, make yourself indispensible. Understand what it is you love about the subject and identify a role that is suitable to that. Then be the best at what you can be.

What has been the biggest lesson in your career to date?

My biggest lesson has been not to give up, to follow a dream and to remain true to my ideals. Many people told me that things weren't possible along the way. I was encouraged to get 'proper jobs' which would have stifled my ambition and imagination. However, I seemed to understand that unless I got to create the type of gardens that I wanted to and unless I explored the reasons for wanting to do things that were different within my own head, I would be left deeply unsatisfied. So following a single vision was important for me.

If you had a motto, what would it be?
My motto would be 'Believe in yourself.'

What advice would you give your 16-year-old self?
I would tell my younger self that I would have to go through all types of turbulence to create a foundation for what would happen next. There's no point being offered everything on a plate. It's important to get out and dig and understand soil while hanging on to dreams. It's important to learn a little a bit of how business works. It's important to understand that good manners are essential. It's important – even at the age of 16 – to turn up on time, to be accommodating, to be pleasant in any situation and, most important, it's important not to waver in your dreams.

❖

Communicating with Your Teen

We have two ears and one mouth so that we can listen twice as much as we speak.

EPICTETUS

As a parent of a teenager, one of the biggest challenges can be communication. Teenagers are in a process of self-discovery, testing boundaries and finding their way in the world. Your natural desire as a parent is to see your children survive and thrive in the years ahead. The focus on the importance of education and choices made at this stage can lead to a confused, concerned and sometimes controlling parent. Ultimately, it is your teenager who has to make the decisions about their future; therefore, it is important that the lines of communication between you are open. Your teen needs to be able to listen to and trust their own inner voice with regard to choices that suit who they really are as an individual.

Engaging Co-operation

At times engaging co-operation from your teen can be a challenge. There are ways to communicate in a way that draws the best out of your teen and reduces conflict. The list below of 'what not to do', which is adapted from the book *How to Talk So Teens Will Listen and Listen So Teens Will Talk* by Adele Faber and Elaine Mazlish, may help you in your everyday interactions. It highlights what does not work and why. With the help of parent coach Marian Byrne,

I have added positive and constructive examples of 'what to do' instead. This may help you in your many conversations with your teen about study, attitude and choices.

DOS AND DON'TS

Don't blame and accuse – they may withdraw or counterattack:	☹ You always leave your homework until the last minute. ☹ You never think beyond the next text or chat with your friends!
Positive alternatives:	☺ I notice that when you leave your homework to the last minute you get very stressed out. Is that something you would like to change? ☺ I know that your friends are really important to you and that's great. What do you think is the best way to balance time with them and get the work you need to do done?
Don't use threats – they won't work after a while if you don't follow through, and if you do follow through, you may just get defiance or sullen compliance:	☹ If you don't start taking this seriously, you're grounded until you do! ☹ If you're not ready to go in five minutes, I'm going without you.
Constructive alternatives:	☺ It is important that you do X. I expect you to take it seriously and do it. ☺ It's really important that we're on time and I would appreciate your co-operation.

17

Commands will get defiance or sullen compliance:	☹ You sit down and get your homework done now! ☹ You'd better start thinking about how you're going to earn a living.
Instead offer them choices:	☺ Are you going to do your homework now or after tea? ☺ We need to look at some career options for you. Would you like to do it now or on Saturday morning?
If you lecture and moralise they will tune out:	☹ If you don't start putting time and effort into your schoolwork, you'll go nowhere. ☹ I'm not going to be looking after you and ferrying you around for the next ten years, so you have to start thinking about …
Instead, encourage them and show them that you support them:	☺ Putting time and effort into your work will pay off in the long run and help you get what you want. ☺ I'm here to support and guide you in whatever way I can.
Warnings won't work after a while:	☹ If you don't study, you're going to fail/do badly in your exam. ☹ If you don't work harder at your Irish, you'll never be able to study teaching.
Instead, ask them to consider and be responsible for the consequences of their choices:	☺ What do you think the outcome might be if you don't do your best? ☺ I know you really want to do teaching. In that context, how important is it to get an honour in Irish?

Being a martyr will either make them tune out or feel guilty:	☹	Are you trying to break my heart?
	☹	I spend all my time looking after you and driving you around and the one time I ask you to do something to help, you make a big fuss about it.
	☹	After all I've done for you ...
	☹	I've spent hours doing all this research and you don't care or appreciate it.
Instead, explain to them honestly and unemotionally how their actions are affecting you:	☺	When you don't clear up after yourself, I feel like you're expecting me to do it, as if it is my job!
	☺	Your co-operation would mean a lot to me. I feel that our relationship would be better if there was more give and take.
	☺	I've invested a lot of time and energy into you because I love you. I've noticed, however, that sometimes I do more than is good for you or me. As a teenager I know you are now much more capable than when you were four and you can do these things for yourself.
Sarcasm lowers their self-esteem and confidence and can damage your relationship with them:	☹	Yes, spending hours on Facebook is really going to prepare you well for your exams/the real world.
Instead, make comments that can help them move forward:	☺	I know you love Facebook. You spend a lot of time on it and if there was an exam in it, I reckon you would get top marks (*remember to use a light, not sarcastic tone*). It just shows how the time you put into something really pays off. In relation to your study, how is that the same?

Comparisons can lower self-esteem and create resentment towards the other person/child/sibling:	☹ Why can't you be more like your sister? ☹ Why can't you be more like your friend Seán? He studies for two hours a night. ☹ When I was your age I …
Instead acknowledge your teen's strengths and help them to work on their weaknesses in a positive manner:	☺ You have your strengths and your sister has hers – each of you is unique. ☺ What habits or steps could you take to move closer to what you want? ☺ When I was young I found it hard to focus too.

Parent coach Marian Byrne suggests keeping these three points in mind when you are trying to engage your teen in co-operation and constructive communication. They are vital:

1. Be present when you are with your teen.
2. Offer them choices, not ultimatums.
3. Listen.

1. Be present when you are present

Sometimes we are present in body but our mind is elsewhere. Our work, worries, the phone, or an endless to-do list can distract us. Our teenagers will know when we are genuinely interested and when we are just going through the motions. We often spend too much time going over what they have done in the **past**, going over times when they let us down. Alternatively, we may be solely focused on the result of the process (the outcome that *you*, the parent, want) or the implications of what will happen if they don't go to college, get into the course they want, etc. We might even threaten that they will end up jobless in the future if they don't get their act together. We are in the **future**. The ideal scenario is to focus on the **present**, and this is not always easy. When we focus on the process in hand and the present, we can:

- Accept that 'we are where we are'. It is good to reflect and learn from the past (what worked well, what did not work), but then we need to move on. There are always opportunities to start afresh. The past is history and what we do today will determine what happens tomorrow.

- Recognise that this stage of your teenager's life can be an opportunity for you to strengthen your relationship with them (it is possible!) instead of being a challenge. Create moments to improve the relationship by spending quality time one to one.

- When we are present, we are more likely to be non-judgemental and that is the most powerful thing we can bring to the process. We are neither judging them by the past nor stressing our concern and anxiety about the future.

- Notice in the present moment and comment when you see improvements, a good attitude or work well done.

2. Offer choices, not ultimatums

Whether we are children, teenagers or adults, it is important for our confidence and self-esteem to feel that we have some control over our environment and ourselves.

This is why as parents we often get so frustrated that our teen won't put the time or effort into their schoolwork. When communicating with your teenager, try to offer them choices within the boundaries of what is acceptable to you. It is a great way of engaging their co-operation and helping them feel empowered in the process.

In thinking of options, remember that the choices need to be:
- respectful of you
- respectful of them
- respectful of what needs to be done.

Here are a few examples of how this might work:
- *We need to spend some time going through the subject choices for next year. Do you want to do it after school one evening this week, or at the weekend?* (Choice)
- *Because you have to give extra time and focus to your schoolwork this year* (a statement, so this is a given), *what can I do that would be of most help to you during this year?* (Choice)
- *I can see that you really enjoy linking up with your friends and that it's very important to you.* (Acknowledgement)

3. Listening

It's vitally important to know how to actively listen to what your child is saying and to ask them the right questions. Most of us like to think that we are good listeners, but in reality, some of our listening skills may leave a lot to be desired. When someone is genuinely and actively listened to, they feel really heard and understood and it is powerful for their self-esteem and confidence. Some people are naturally good listeners and others may have to make a conscious effort to listen actively or at a deep level.

Often we are listening but doing something else at the same time (driving, on the computer, cooking). We may *hear* what they say, but do they experience being listened to?

Not all teenagers are articulate; often they don't know what they mean or want until they actually say it. As a parent, it is important to take the time to help them think things through and identify options in a way that builds your relationship with them and develops their life and thinking skills.

Coaches use a number of listening techniques, but if you remember just these two tips, communication with your teen should improve.

> **Listening Tip 1: Listen with your eyes, ears, heart and undivided attention.**

This is a complete way of listening that picks up on all the information available and encourages your teen to open up. Using your eyes means that you see facial expressions and body language. Using your ears means that you hear not only the words they say but also their tone, pauses, etc. Listening with your heart (being empathetic) and giving your undivided attention (being present) are both important for their self-esteem and confidence, and an invitation to keep talking.

Here are some tips on how to listen completely:

- Stop what you are doing, sit down or turn towards them so they know they have your full attention. This is not always appropriate or necessary, but it is powerful.
- If your mobile phone is on, turn it off. If it rings and you don't answer it, it gives a clear message that they are your priority.
- Nodding your head, looking attentive, saying 'I see', 'Uh huh', etc. lets them know that you are listening and this encourages them to keep talking.
- Repeat back or paraphrase what they say. Again, this shows that you are listening; and hearing you repeat what they have said can help them reflect on what they have said in a different way. It offers the chance to clarify.
- Offering observations is another way of raising their awareness.
- Try coming at them from the side door by talking to them while engaging in a task such as cooking, tinkering with an engine or decorating a room.

- Allow them to be the teacher. Ask them to show you how to use an app, play a computer game, apply make-up or teach you teenage slang! Start talking about the task in hand and before you know it, they will go off the subject and open up.
- If your teenager is uncomfortable sitting and talking face to face, try going for a walk side by side in the open air. This often makes it easier for them to communicate.
- If you are in the car with them, it's a great opportunity to turn your time as 'taxi driver' into key communication time and it works very well. There is no eye contact, there are fewer distractions for both of you (assuming that you can drive safely and converse at the same time), the car is a safe, neutral space and a drive takes place over a limited period of time.

> **Listening Tip 2: Ask open questions.**

Open questions invite others to 'tell their story' in their own words. Closed questions are those that elicit a 'yes' or 'no' answer. The following examples contrast open versus closed questions. While the subject being discussed is the same, the answers will be different depending on the questions the parent asks. Compare the following approaches to the same question:

- **Closed question:** Do you want to go to college?
- **Open question:** What are your thoughts on going to college?

Other examples of open questions:

- How can I help you with …?
- What elements of architecture/cooking/social work, etc. appeal to you?
- What do you want to do next?
- Why are you having a hard time with this?
- What's going on?

- What can I do to relieve the pressure?
- Help me understand ...
- How would you like things to be different?
- What do you want to do next?

Affirmations

Affirmations are statements that affirm or acknowledge your teenager's strengths, no matter how big or small. Affirmations can help your teen believe in their ability to change as well as build self-confidence and self-esteem. They must be used in a genuine way otherwise your teen will sense the phoniness and will back off.

Examples of affirming responses:
- You bring up a good point.
- You handled that situation well.
- That's very considerate of you.
- You were a great help to me.
- That's a useful suggestion.
- When I was your age, I'm not sure if I would have managed X as well.
- You have ability in ...
- That's enterprising of you.

Think of affirming responses you could use with your teenager.

Reflective Listening

Both adults and children want to know that they are being heard and understood. This is especially important when communicating with teenagers. The best way to let people know that you 'hear' them is to reflect back to them what they have said. This is called 'reflective listening' and it enhances communication and understanding immensely.

Teenagers are not always the clearest or most eloquent communicators, using responses such as 'dunno' or 'whatever'. Nevertheless, they still want to feel understood. The deepest form of listening and connecting with your teen is to use empathy. Empathise with the emotion they are displaying/feeling and reflect that feeling back to them, showing that you understand what they are going through.

Statement	I should do something about getting work experience.
Repetition	'Do something.' 'Do something about work experience.'
Same meaning, slightly different words	'Do something about finding experience in the world of work.'
Reflections of meaning	'Finding work experience is a problem.' 'Work experience would help.' 'You could try harder.'
Reflections of feelings	'You are concerned about finding work experience. It's important to you.' 'You haven't been putting your heart into finding work experience.'

Parents who used these techniques found them useful, even though they took some time to get used to them. One parent told me that she found that these communication techniques opened up a good, honest dialogue with her daughter. Her daughter revealed how frustrated she was with learning and that she wanted to pursue a more practical career such as being a beautician, and sharing her concerns gave her a great sense of relief.

Enhancing Your Teen's Confidence

Every parent wants their teenager to be confident and make choices that will lead to future happiness and success. The level of confidence your teenager has will determine where they set their sights in terms of their career and life goals. So how can you improve your child's confidence?

Remember!
The longest journey is made up of small steps.

Small Steps

A useful starting point is to consider ways of increasing your child's existing confidence and to treat their development as a journey. This development can be compared to climbing a mountain. Help them on their climb by acknowledging their achievements and good results, whether personal or academic. Each action they take is a contribution to their overall success along their journey.

For a shy teenager, a small step might be going into a shop to buy something or picking up the telephone to make a call. Get them used to the idea that small steps change everything and that repeating positive actions on a continuous basis can help achieve a good outcome. For example, constructive action around study or getting organised in their school life can contribute to better results. Equally, healthy eating and exercise habits can produce a positive outcome in their overall performance.

Focus on strengths and find the 'gold' within your child.

In my experience, the best place to begin is focusing on your child's strengths and helping them find the 'star' within. Let them know why you admire, love and like them. This can be associated with an achievement, an event, a kind gesture or an obstacle they overcame. Point out what seems to be working well for them and what they are doing well.

> Studies show that by the time we are eighteen years old, we will have been praised, supported and encouraged about 25,000 times. 50% of these occasions will have been before the age of three! By the time we reach eighteen, we will have been criticised, scolded, belittled, and told we are stupid around 225,000 times. No wonder many people grow up with a negative mindset that they keep for the rest of their lives! As a parent you have the power to boost your child's positive mindset and self-esteem.
>
> (Nick Williams, *The Work We Were Born To Do*)

Teenagers are often obsessed with their appearance. They worry about their size, body shape, height, clothes, spots and their overall image. Therefore, as much as possible, compliment their inner selves, their integrity, enthusiasm, determination, and self-control. Focus your praise on the person they are and encourage them to appreciate their qualities, values and personality. Relate these qualities to the world of work, for example by saying things like 'Employers are always looking for enthusiasm and I can see that you approach all your tasks enthusiastically. Your attitude will be greatly valued in the future'; or 'I can see that you were very determined and focused in the way you approached that match. That determination will take you far in the future.'

Even if it is sometimes hard to point out strengths, try to find the 'gold' in what they are doing. As a guidance counsellor, I'm often challenged in class by a student seeking constant attention or making unnecessary remarks. In these situations, I respond by saying, 'that is a unique and creative way of looking at things', and I try to find the 'gold' in the student. Even if a teenager is weak academically, I will point out their social skills, kindness or willingness to help out. As much as possible, I try to link it to the world of work. It could even be something like, 'I noticed that you took the initiative to help out there and initiative is something that all employers are looking for.'

TASK A: FIND THE GOLD AND POLISH IT

Find ways to compliment your teenager that will highlight their strengths and add value to them. Uncover the gold within them even if your child presents with challenging behaviour. Let them hear you compliment them to someone else. Emphasise the effort they make rather than their intelligence.

Look for and comment on the positive behaviour and characteristics of your child. The following words may act as prompts:

> clever, insightful, useful, thoughtful, caring, innovative, practical, hardworking, generous, wise, patient, flexible, effective, supportive, healthy, dependable, attentive, perceptive, skilled, articulate, careful, considerate, organised, expert, gentle, invaluable, interesting, kind, quick-thinking ...

For example:

Teen: Dad, I called around to the local Spar to see if there were any summer jobs.

Parent: That's very mature of you; calling in to the shop shows that you have real initiative.

Teen: I spoke with a student who is on an animation course to find out what the course might be like.

Parent: It's very responsible of you to research your courses in advance.

Teen: I don't think there will be any jobs out there for me when I finish college.

Parent: I know you have the drive and enthusiasm to create your own opportunities regardless of the jobs market.

Think of some supportive responses to these statements:

- 'I practised taking notes in class and it really worked.'
- 'Today I started my new fitness programme and I feel it might help me study.'
- 'I rang a small business and asked for work experience.'
- 'I've decided to participate in the Gaisce Project.'
- 'I'm really stressed about the Leaving Cert and I'm not sure if it will go well for me.'
- 'Everyone in the school production thinks I'm shy.'

Adapted from Winning New Jobs, a job search programme developed by the Social Research Department, University of Michigan.

Communication is the bedrock on which career conversations are made. Good communication skills can help you get beyond moody, monosyllabic responses such as 'dunno', 'whatever', or the grunting sounds some teenagers make. Getting the communication flowing between you and your teen is vital to opening up a world of possibilities. As your teenager develops and grows as a person and their self-concept changes, so too will their ideas about themselves in relation to the world of work.

Step 1 Key Points

- Engage the co-operation of your teenager.
- Offer them choices, not ultimatums.
- Be present to them.
- Begin a dialogue with them about their career.
- Listen and respond effectively.

MY CAREER

Dr Ria Mahon, MD, MRCPI, MPH
Medical Officer, Irish Medicines Board

The Irish Medicines Board, or Health Products Regulatory Authority (HPRA) protects and enhances public and animal health through the regulation of health products.

'Just do it!'

How did your career in medicine begin?
I had a background interest in science; however, I knew that I needed to be interacting with people rather than carrying out experiments in a lab. When I repeated my Leaving Cert, I had a very clear vision and the determination to study medicine. I absolutely loved the idea of the challenge of medicine.

Did you always want to do what you do now?
There is a great variety in what I do now in regulatory medicine. I started out my career in hospital medicine. Hospital medicine was very rewarding, especially working in

medicine of the elderly (formerly geriatrics), but I realised that maintaining a work/life balance going forward would have been very difficult. So in 1999 I made the tough decision to study a master's in Public Health and get into the preventive side of medicine. This decision made sense to me as I love medicine and interacting with the public and it allowed more life/work balance. After my master's, I went on to work for the Irish Medical Board. Along the way, I took a career break from 2007 to 2011. During this time my husband, Ian, and I worked together and formed Horizon Speakers, which taught me business skills and furthered my people skills. My career has unfolded in unexpected and interesting ways!

What do you enjoy most about what you do now?
Currently, I am working with the safety aspect of medical devices and it is totally new and innovative. These devices include cardiac valves and prosthetic hips and have a huge impact on the quality of people's health all over the world. You cannot stop innovation or new ideas and it is an exciting part of medicine to be involved in.

What is the toughest thing about your job?
The toughest thing about my job is ensuring the right balance between knowing the detail of the job and making sure to make a clear decision based on all the facts presented. In other words, while knowing the detail, it is important not to lose sight of the bigger picture and to make clear, decisive decisions based on all the facts presented. This is very important when deciding the benefit/risk of a medicinal product or medical device.

What motivates you?
What motivates me every day is really myself; it's important to

realise that if it's meant to be it's up to me! Over the years what has helped me realise this are the great books I have read and the inspirational people I have met and listened to.

Who or what inspired you along the way?
Inspirations along the way include my teachers at school – some of them made me realise that I was able to get through the exams; my parents were always supportive; and later in college, there was a good collegial group in my class and we studied together. It's important to get around like-minded people and stay away from people who do not encourage you in your goals and dreams.

What advice on getting started would you give young people who want a career in the same field?
Be brave and follow the career that really motivates you. Do not follow a job path just for financial gain as this could lead you to a very frustrating and unfulfilled life. Find what you enjoy and find a way to make a living from this. Remember that fortune favours the brave. Be persistent in following your goals and dreams, as there will always be obstacles in your way. Sometimes how you reach your dreams will not always be clear to you. Focus on the end result and the way will sort itself out. Remember that hard work gets you a long way and that success is 99 per cent perspiration.

What has been the biggest lesson in your career to date?
The change of direction – going from hospital medicine to public health/regulatory medicine – as new skills and new ways of working had to be learned. One small example would be that I quickly had to become very familiar with Excel sheets and proficient in the use of computers, which

I hadn't really had to use during my clinical years at Cork University Hospital. However, I'm always up to a challenge!

If you had a motto, what would it be?
Just do it!

What advice would you give your 16-year-old self?
I was a shy, quiet 16-year-old, but I knew that the world was full of possibilities! Remember that you don't have to be the most outgoing, well-spoken individual to do very well; you can learn those traits along the way. Just take action, make decisions, keep on your path, and keep ploughing on; you will be amazed at what you can achieve.

Remember, we overestimate what we can do in a year but underestimate what we can do in a decade. Best of luck and enjoy yourself along the way.

❖

STEP 2

Choosing a Career They'll Love

You've got to find what you love, and that is as true for your work as it is for your lovers. And the only way to do great work is to love what you do. If you haven't found it yet, keep looking. Don't settle. As with all matters of the heart, you'll know when you find it.

STEVE JOBS

The second step is 'choosing a career you love'. It is central to your child's future wellbeing and happiness that they focus on choosing a career that they will love. We all know and recognise people who are unhappy in their work. Many of us have been brought up with a puritanical notion of work – that work has to be hard and is something to be endured. Some of us view work as a necessary evil, a means to an end and just a way of paying the bills. Others really enjoy our work.

The people interviewed for this book all love the work they do and are following their passions. Some recognised their calling and the work they were born to do at a young age. The majority, however, found what they loved along the way. It is worth noting that some of the people interviewed took an apprenticeship or followed specialist training that did not involve going to university. What is clear from all the interviews is that the people interviewed are dedicated to their craft and to providing an excellent service.

There are no hard and fast rules about finding the work that you love. However, in his book *The Element*, Sir Ken Robinson emphasises the value of finding your passion. He offers us clues on how to uncover 'the Element'.

> The Element has two main features, and there are two conditions for being in it. The features are aptitude and passion. The conditions are attitude and opportunity. The sequence goes something like this: I get it; I love it; I want it; Where is it? (Ken Robinson, *The Element*, p. 22)

'I get it' refers to having a natural ability for something. 'I love it' is a passion for something. 'I want it' is the desire and drive to achieve something. 'Where is it?' refers to the curiosity to seek out opportunities that allow the development or unfolding of a passion.

As a parent, your main job is to help your child to listen to their heart, their gut, their true selves and to notice the times when they feel on course, on track or when they are doing something that they truly love. Encourage your teen to notice the tasks and activities that give them energy and to pay attention to the tasks that drain their energy. Energy levels offer great insights into true passions and can be indicators of a suitable career direction. Their task is to discover who they truly are. This is a process that takes time and that evolves as they grow. It will require patience from you to step back and facilitate conversations that allow for self-enquiry. Your teenager may change their mind over and over again about what they love, or they may stick fast to a long-held dream.

Emily's Story

Emily Hillier loved baking and as a 16-year-old liked to spend all her time trying out new recipes. I first met her when she was picking her subjects for the Leaving Cert and looking for

Transition Year (TY) work experience. Her love for baking had made a strong impression on me. Years afterwards, I wondered about Emily's journey and I followed her up at age 20. She recounted the value of work experience for her career direction as follows:

'Right now I have just completed my first year of a degree in Bakery and Pastry Management in DIT. Although I got into Trinity College Dublin to study history and geography, I went with my gut and stayed true to my love of baking. It was a tough decision, but I am happy I had the courage to choose baking.

'Looking back, it was my work experience in Transition Year in Avoca that really helped me make up my mind about my career path. It started off as two weeks and they kept me on for three months. The school was very supportive of me in extending my experience. This experience expanded my entire knowledge of baking. I started work at six a.m., worked until three p.m., and had to learn to structure and plan my day. It taught me time management and the value of preparation and planning. As I was the only person under eighteen years of age in Avoca, this made me come out of my shell and gave me the confidence to talk to people. It was a real validation for me to be told by professional bakers that I had talent.

'My first year in DIT was both brilliant and challenging. For the summer, I am juggling two jobs and I have a great offer waiting in the wings. My vision for my future is to travel and learn different baking techniques across the world. It is my dream to open up my own business and I am continually inspired by the Taste of Dublin and Bloom Festival. Food is really celebrated these days!'

Emily's advice to parents and teenagers is to really explore the value of work experience.

'My friend Emma did her experience in a school and that confirmed her desire to study to be a science teacher and my friend Katie went to a hospital and is now studying nursing. It is a trial and error process; try as many things as you can and explore as much as you can, until you stumble upon your path.'

In Step 2, you as a parent will:

- Discover techniques for identifying passions and areas of interest
- Learn how to rank those interests in importance
- Learn how to help your teen explore careers related to those interests
- Learn how to encourage your teenager to think outside the box in relation to their career
- Explore the idea of a portfolio career.

Identifying Passions and Areas of Interest

Your teenager came into this world as a unique package of talents, gifts and resources. Their job is to find out what they love doing, to specialise and excel in that area and to serve the world with their unique set of talents. As Aristotle said, 'Where your talents and the needs of the world cross, your calling can be found.'

Accept that your teenager has their own unique interests rather than comparing them to others in the family. If your teen doesn't seem to have a passion, encourage them to create a passion. Tell them not to overthink things, just to try out new things and move beyond their comfort zone. Suggest that they follow their curiosity and see where it leads them. Where possible, get them to seek new opportunities to expand their interests and views of themselves. Finally, give them permission to follow a career path they love.

Although you may have a great interest in sport and want your child to be an athlete, your child might have a greater interest in music; so allow them to have their own interests. Be mindful not to impose your own career goals or unlived dreams on your child. When choices and decisions are made for young people, they often grow up into adults full of self-doubt. The most supportive thing you can do as a parent is offer some guidelines that will help them explore the career options open to them. Frequently, teenagers cannot see their own strengths and personal qualities and may even discount their interests as possible sources of income in the future. Some teenagers don't realise that it is possible to make money from their interests, for example computer games or cars.

One of the best ways to clarify underlying passions and interests is to sit down with your teen and ask them the following open-ended questions. Jot down notes on their answers.

School subjects:
- What subjects do they enjoy most?
- What grabs their attention and inspires them? Look for common themes.

Outside school:
- What sections in bookshops capture their interest?
- What do they read about for pleasure?
- What websites do they enjoy browsing (apart from social media sites)?

Skills that come naturally to them:
- What skills come to your teen without thought or effort?
- What skills did they enjoy using in a part-time job or in Transition Year (TY)?
- What skills did they enjoy developing through An Gaisce (the

President's Award)? (The Gaisce Award is aimed at young people aged 15–25. The word Gaisce refers to achievement. The programme involves four areas of activity: community involvement, personal skills, physical recreation and adventure. The awards are given at bronze, silver and gold levels. See www. gaisce.org for more details. The UK equivalent of the award is the Prince's Trust Award.)

Activities that are fun, enjoyable and give energy:
- What type of places, things, people and activities give you energy?
- When do you feel most alive?

Voluntary, community, club and service activities:
- What type of voluntary work do/did you enjoy?
- When have you helped in your community and found it satisfying?
- What roles in your local sports club have you enjoyed?
- Have you taken on any roles at school (e.g. prefect, mentor, parts in school plays/musicals, etc.)?

When your teenager has completed the list, use the following chart to prioritise their favourite subjects.

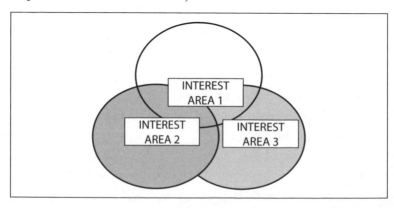

You can use this template to narrow down the main areas of interest and gain clarity about where these two or three areas overlap. When I did this exercise for myself, my three areas were guidance, creativity and Japanese. With a group of colleagues, we brainstormed the endless career possibilities these led to, which left me considering options that had never crossed my mind before. For example: writing about education and guidance; teaching English in Japan; being a guidance counsellor; working in a museum, such as the Chester Beatty Library, which specialises in Oriental art, etc.

Below is an example from one of my students.

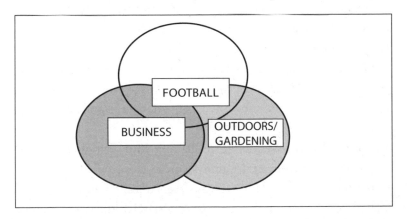

If he were your child, you would encourage him to think of ways to combine all his loves. He could ask family, friends and other adults to brainstorm possibilities in a creative way and, of course, the internet always provides a host of possibilities. Suggestions might include sports manager/coaching; starting a business maintaining football grounds; creating products for soccer; working for a professional soccer club, etc. This particular student went on to do a Business Management and Sports Coaching course and he earned money during the summer doing landscape gardening.

To return to the questions around interest clarification: When you have jotted down the interests that your teen has identified, have them decide which suggestions appeal to them most and get them to explore them further by having conversations with people who are working in their area of interest. If this style doesn't suit your child, perhaps the section 'Knowing Yourself' under Further Resources at the end of this book would help clarify their interests. Some teenagers draw a blank whenever they think of the future. If you ask them what they want to do they typically answer, 'I don't know'. In these instances, it is easier to make a list of jobs or work environments they *don't* like in order to find work situations they *do* like. Most teenagers are sure of what they hate or don't like. They might say, 'I don't want to be in an office' or 'I don't want to work with blood', which would rule out most medical posts; or they might say 'I don't want to be in one place every day', which is a prompt to explore jobs that involve movement, travel and variety.

A **contrast list** is a useful tool for helping your teen discover what they *do* want. A contrast list allows you to compare what you like with what you do not like. If your teen doesn't know what they want, often the easiest place to start is with what they *don't* want or like. Here is an example based on my own preferences:

CLARITY THROUGH CONTRAST

Contrast	Clarity
Things I don't like to do:	*Things I do like to do:*
Working with animals	Organising events
Working in the same place all the time	Meeting new people
Having to do the same thing every day	Reading
Anything to do with blood	Teaching

Maths	French and German
Working with my hands	Getting dressed up
Vet	Driving
Technical work	Travel agent
Working in a hospital	Travelling
Working on my own	Tour guide

Have your teen make their own list using the template below:

Contrast	Clarity
Things I don't like to do:	*Things I do like to do:*

Portfolio Careers

Emphasise that a career doesn't need to be an either/or choice. Your teen could do a number of jobs at the same time and pursue what is known as a *portfolio career*. Having a portfolio career means that you work part-time on several different jobs instead of having a single full-time job. It is also a way of working that can incorporate all your career interests so that you do not have to sacrifice one interest for another.

I once met a young man who was torn between becoming a wildlife ranger and a nurse. He loved the idea of the freedom of the outdoors and caring for wildlife in a national park. He also wanted to help others and to make a difference to people who were sick by using his empathic skills. In the end, he became a volunteer with the wildlife rangers in the local national park and went on to study nursing. Along the way, he trained as a mountain leader and in wildlife and took groups on paid tours in the national park. In his spare time, he reared birds of prey as a small business. In this way, he was able to combine all his loves into his work life.

I often meet college students who combine their interests by coaching and tutoring, setting up consultancy businesses *and* studying at PhD level. Consider with your teenager all possible opportunities that combining their career interests could offer. Even if your teen is unsure where their real interests lie, ask them to keep noticing what they enjoy in their everyday lives and to think of ways of making a living from doing what they most love. Finally, it takes great courage to follow what you love, particularly when it comes to the arts (music, art, writing, performance, etc.). The creative arts are often viewed as an area where it is impossible to make a living. There are many people out there who will dissuade and discourage young people from following what is in their hearts. Some young people are afraid to voice their dreams and keep them locked inside. Sometimes they feel safer doing this.

I once worked with a young man who had a very deep desire to work in sound and music production, but this idea was locked away in the privacy of his own mind. It took some encouragement to draw it out of him, to validate his future image, and then to explore suitable music production courses.

Sometimes young people have to deal with their own internal dialogue and fear around following their passions. Recently I worked with a Leaving Cert student who had always wanted to become a primary school teacher. She was afraid, though, that because of the high points requirement she might be setting herself up for a fall. Therefore, she convinced herself it was unattainable and that events management was a more achievable target. She had no interest at all in events management. I looked at her original dream and passion for young people and got her to reconnect with the feeling of the dream and the future reality of being a primary school teacher. We explored alternative routes into teaching that involved lower points and less pressure. We looked at building a more positive mindset around her ambition to become a primary teacher. We also discussed alternative routes into primary teaching, including graduate entry routes. All this helped her to stay true to following a career that she knew she would love.

As a parent you can be a dream builder. Young people often experience 'dream bashers', voices telling them not to follow their hearts, not to aim high, not to take risks, not to be creative and to choose safe options. (The terms 'dream-builder' and 'dream-basher' are used by Nick Williams in his book *Powerful Beyond Measure*.) Too many people are in jobs they don't like for this reason. As a parent you can help your teen associate with people outside your family who will affirm, support and inspire their passions.

Remember:

Success is not the key to happiness. Happiness is the key to success. If you love what you are doing, you will be successful. (Albert Schweitzer)

Step 2 Key Points

- The first step for your teen in choosing a career they will love is to identify their interests.
- These interests can come from school, hobbies, volunteering or part-time work.
- You can clarify interests using a contrast list.
- A career is not an 'either/or' choice. A portfolio career, which combines many interests and skills, might be suitable for your teen.

MY CAREER

Neven Maguire
Chef and Restaurant Owner
www.macneanrestaurant.com

Neven is the owner of MacNean House, Restaurant and Cookery School in Blacklion, Co Cavan. McNean's is considered Ireland's leading restaurant and has received many prestigious awards. Neven regularly makes TV and radio appearances.

'Get experience, show respect, enjoy and love what you do.'

How did your career as a chef begin?

I started cooking with my Mum in the kitchen at a very early age. She never pushed me into it. She just saw that I was interested and showed me things. She encouraged me and she judged it right. I went to Fermanagh College after my Junior Cert. I loved college! And I loved it again when I taught there some years later.

Did you always want to do what you do now?
Yes! From a very young age I always knew that this was what I wanted to do. You spend so many years working that I think it is important to like what you do.

What do you enjoy most about what you do now?
Everything! I love the huge variety – from cooking in my kitchen to my TV work to my books. My work is exciting and varied. I feel so lucky to look forward to going to the kitchen each day and working with people I like and who take pride in what they do.

What is the toughest thing about your job?
Every day I learn something different; my job is very rewarding. You get used to the long hours, you have to put your heart and soul into what you do to be on top of your game. You have to remember that you are as good as your last meal and every day brings new customers and they all deserve the best that you can do.

What motivates you?
My customers, family, my staff and good seasonal produce. I love chatting with customers and I learn from them all the time.

Who or what inspired you along the way?
My catering lecturer, my home economics teacher in school ... I have been inspired by many people I have worked with ... Paul Rankin, Lea Linster and many more. For television, I got the best grounding possible with Marty Whelan and Mary Kennedy on *Open House*.

What advice on getting started would you give young people who want a career in the same field?

Go and work in a kitchen, get experience, show respect, enjoy and love what you do. The hours are long, so if you don't really want to do it, make it your hobby and not your job. It is not a job where you can have 'off' days. You have to pay attention to detail each and every day.

What has been the biggest lesson in your career to date?

I like to learn something different every day. But one of the lessons I have learned is that your staff are very important. My chefs love food as much as I do and we travel together to sample great restaurants. It feels great to lead a team that wants to excel and is proud of its work.

If you had a motto what would it be?

Love what you do!

What advice would you give your 16-year-old self?

Looking back, it would probably be to manage my time better. I took on too much at times and it is important to prioritise what matters in work and family life. I think it was only when we had our children that I realised how important time management is. But then, I wouldn't have achieved the level of success I enjoy without a lot of long hours.

❖

Help Your Teenager Identify their Skills

When love and skill work together, expect a masterpiece.

CHARLES READE

Your career conversations with your teen need to focus on their skills. Helping your teen focus on their skills will help them become more aware of what they have to offer. Taking account of your teen's natural strengths will empower them to make good career choices. Many teenagers and adults freeze when they hear the word 'skills' and will often say, 'I haven't any skills.' By using the tools and exercises in this step, you will help your teen draw out and become conscious of natural skills and strengths they didn't realise they had.

Step 3:

- Provides you with a method for classifying your teenager's skills into four categories of career area preferences
- Includes exercises to help your teenager become aware of their own skills
- Introduces the skills valued by employers
- Looks at the skills that give your teenager great energy and joy
- Examines ways in which your teen can develop and build their skills through community involvement, volunteering, etc.
- Stresses the importance of introducing 'flow' or 'following your bliss' in work.

Many adults and teenagers can't identify their strengths and skills, yet they are keenly aware of their weaknesses. Sometimes it takes others – even people outside the family – to point out their unique skills.

Data, Ideas, People, Things

A 'skill' is a capacity to do something well. They are developed over time. Skills generally fall into four categories: skills with **data**; skills with **ideas**; **people** skills; and skills with **things**. These categories are sometimes known as DIPT for short. The chart below, adapted from the book *What Color is Your Parachute?* by Richard Nelson Bolles, clarifies what these categories mean:

WHAT ARE SKILLS?

Category	Examples
Data	Recording, working with figures, systems, routines, record-keeping, organising information, bringing together facts, memorising, co-ordinating, calculating, editing, analysing, estimating, compiling, computing, copying, comparing
Ideas	Designing, interpreting, abstract thinking, creating, problem-solving, language skills, composing music, planning, innovating, writing, colour co-ordination, brainstorming ideas, enterprising, observing, improvising, challenging ideas
People	Informing, teaching, persuading, motivating, selling, mentoring, negotiating, instructing, supervising, questioning, listening, counselling, leading, mediating, organising people, serving, hosting, taking instructions, helping

Things	Making, repairing, transporting, using tools, using hands, balance, co-ordination, setting up, precision working/working with tools or instruments that require accuracy (draughtsperson/lab technician/using medical equipment), operating, preparing food, typing, playing sport, lifting, building, driving, manipulating, tending, feeding, handling

When I meet teenagers for the first time, I ask them off the top of their heads to put *data, ideas, people* and *things* in order of their preference. Ask your child what their order of preference would be. This will prompt insights and suggest what balance of work with information, ideas, people and things they want. Some may realise that they want to work alone; others may want to be with other people all the time; others may love to work with their hands or objects.

Keep in mind that many skills are transferable. This means that they can be used in a variety of different jobs and are therefore skills that employers will look for. The following is a list of skills desired by employers, which may serve as an extra aid in helping teenagers identify their skills. Research carried out by the 2006 Transferable Skills Project (www.skillsproject.ie/integrate/whyintegrate.html) identified the following skills as the most important for graduates in their careers:

1. Oral communication
2. Time management
3. Teamwork
4. Presentation skills
5. Coping with multiple tasks
6. Managing one's own learning

7. Written communication
8. Planning
9. IT skills
10. Decision-making
11. Problem-solving
12. Critical thinking

Brainstorm your teenager's skills with them (see Task B). For example, if they have worked in a local shop they may have discovered that they like serving customers, helping people, solving problems and using their initiative. Perhaps at school they have discovered that they enjoy analysing information and gathering new data.

TASK B: BRAINSTORMING YOUR TEEN'S SKILLS

Taking the list of skills desired by employers (above), brainstorm on a piece of paper all the ways in which your teenager uses those skills. This will heighten their awareness of their abilities. It is also an opportunity for them to think about which skills and activities give them the most energy. What kinds of activity provide them with an increase in their energy levels? When are they, in Martha Beck's phrase, 'doing without doing', in other words engaging in an activity without thinking too much or forcing it along? What places energise them? Where do they feel most alive? Is it the outdoors, the sea, shopping, airports, garages? Do certain kinds of people inspire them? Get them to write down the top five skills they most enjoy using or things that get them moving, e.g. the school musical, surfing, shopping on a budget, organising a trip.

Energy-giving activities, skills, people or places:

1. _____

2. _____

3. _____

4. _____

5. _____

Look at these responses and see which ones your teen feels most enthusiastic about. Examine how they could further develop these skills in their future career.

Hollie's Story

Hollie Roper is a Transition Year student. Here are the results of her brainstorm of her skills:

1. **Oral communication:** As part of Gaisce (the Presidential Award) Hollie is coaching an under-10s camogie team and encouraging and leading the girls on drills.

2. **Time management:** Work experience in a veterinary practice. This involves getting up early, travelling to the practice, being there on time, adhering to breaks, preparing and cleaning up consultation rooms according to deadlines.

3. **Teamwork:** Playing midfield/full back on the camogie team, pulling together and helping each other out.

4. **Presentation skills:** Hollie made a presentation on the Brandenburg Gate for an Economics and Environment project in TY. Learned how to use PowerPoint. Installed background music into a PowerPoint presentation on Irish music.

5. **Coping with multiple tasks:** Hollie's unsure of when in her life she does this, but as a typical teenager she has a lot of different things going on!

6. **Managing one's own learning:** In preparation for a language exchange to France, she's brushing up on her French in her spare time and takes part in a local French class in the community.

7. **Written communication:** Recording and keeping a reflective diary on Transition Year activities; 'Weebly', a free website.

8. **Planning:** Organising and planning a traditional music performance for Seachtain na Gaeilge; selecting tunes, planning practice sessions and putting a booklet of tunes together.

9. **IT skills:** Hollie's starting to learn IT skills; she needs to learn Microsoft Word.

10. **Decision-making:** Picking subjects for the Leaving Cert, deciding where to go on work experience (she has been very focused on becoming a vet and needs to look at other options), prioritising her time and deciding to give up playing camogie at county level and sticking to club level in order to do other things.

11. **Problem-solving:** Hollie isn't quite sure where she does this.

12. **Critical thinking:** Making a documentary for radio, looking at the topic and the rationale and thinking about sound effects, etc.

These are Hollie's energy-giving activities, places, people and tasks:

1. **Energy-giving activities:** Surfing, a fast camogie match, a drama or music performance.

2. **Energy-giving places:** Shopping for clothes or baking materials, travelling to Florence, looking at architecture and going to places of cultural and artistic interest, the cinema.

3. **Energy-giving people:** Watching talented musicians like Hozier and Queen, watching Roger Federer play tennis.

4. **Energy-giving tasks:** Looking after animals (cats, dogs, rabbits, horses and donkeys); animal welfare; baking cakes and designing and decorating them.

5. **Other energy-givers:** Taking part in any competition, music, drama and quizzes.

Here's Hollie's mind map:

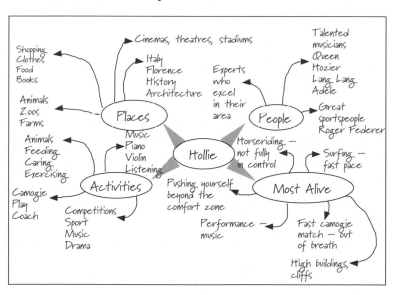

From this discussion, it seems that Hollie feels most alive in a competitive situation that involves performance. She enjoys pushing herself beyond her comfort zone. In exploring various skills, it seems that Hollie would prefer not to work directly with people but rather with animals as a vet. She is willing to explore zoology and other science-related areas such as pharmaceutical science, bio-science, food science, chemical engineering and areas that might involve research. She needs to look into these for her future career. She is motivated by excellence and excels in a competitive environment.

Sitting down with Hollie and asking questions helped increase her awareness of her skills and strengths.

Step into Action!

Successful people are defined by action. The writer Leo Tolstoy once commented that people often told him that they were not sure whether they could write or not as they had never tried. The first task is to take the first step and then the next step, and the next, and continue to take a series of small steps. If we string together a series of small steps, we can climb the mountain and reach our goals. Moving beyond our comfort zone allows us to challenge and uncover our skills. It's important to remember that skills are developed, discovered and polished as we grow as individuals.

In his book *Tycoon*, entrepreneur Peter Jones encourages a commitment to learning inside and outside the classroom. He feels that people inclined to start up businesses are always seeking new information and facts; and they are interested in 'not just academic knowledge but practical knowledge that comes from listening, observing and learning from life itself. If we can open ourselves up to new ideas and new ways of thinking, the world really is our oyster.'

Your teen can make the world their oyster and a place of opportunity by trying something different, developing new skills and taking on new responsibilities and challenges. Perhaps they could create a plan of action. This plan could detail how they plan to develop new skills or improve existing ones by:

- Volunteering in their area of interest, for example with the St Vincent de Paul, Samaritans, Foróige or the local GAA club
- Attending conferences or talks by professional bodies in their area of interest
- Networking – widening their contacts, starting in their own area with friends, family and people in the community; building relationships with beneficial connections
- Getting involved in local community groups and projects
- Going to exhibitions, e.g. the Young Scientist and Technology Exhibition; attending career information days
- Joining Junior Toastmasters, a youth club, a Junior Chamber of Commerce, the Leo Lions club or even a young entrepreneurs' club or the Network for Teaching Entrepreneurship run through Foróige
- Doing a first aid course, joining the Reserve Defence Forces, the Red Cross, the Order of Malta or the Civil Defence
- Going to college open days or shows put on by college students
- Finding a role model or mentor, someone with the experience and knowledge to help your teen develop additional skills and expertise.

Sit down with your teen, draw up a plan together, and think about the skills they would like to develop. Then talk about the steps your teen could take, keeping in mind that skills are developed and grow as we grow. This exercise could be the start of a great discovery for your teen!

- **Skill 1** I wish to develop further: _____

   _____

- Step to be taken: _____

   _____

- **Skill 2** I wish to develop further: _____

   _____

- Step to be taken: _____
_____

- **Skill 3** I wish to develop further: _____
_____

- Step to be taken: _____
_____

One of the most important things to remember about skills is that they can be developed. If your teen is not brilliant at doing something just at the moment, that doesn't mean that they can't improve greatly or even become experts in an area.

By stepping into action, your teen can develop skills, confidence and ability in their areas of interest. Woody Allen said that 80 per cent of success is just turning up. I have seen many teens soar after actively developing their skills by getting part-time work or gaining experience in the areas that interest them. Some were in their element when working with horses, or in a Garda station or working with children with special needs. These teens were in what the psychologist Mihaly Csikszentmihalyi refers to as 'flow'. In other words, they found pleasure and satisfaction in activities that brought about a state of heightened focus.

An Olympic skater described 'flow' as what happens when you feel a rush and your body merges with the music. Flow might be found in playing the piano, creating art, playing football, working with children, working out maths problems, or helping others.

Joseph Campbell, a lifelong student of human behaviour and mythology, articulated a similar idea when he spoke about 'following your bliss', which means identifying the pursuit or activity that you are truly passionate about and giving yourself completely to it. In doing this, you will find your fullest potential and serve your community to the greatest possible extent. This is what American sociologist and author of *Finding Your Own North*

Star Martha Beck refers to in her book as 'the times where they "are doing without doing" with zest and delight ... in these moments, career miracles begin!'

Step 3 Key Points

- We all have skills relating to data, ideas, people and things (DIPT).
- Skills can be developed and polished and they grow as we grow.
- Skills can be developed in school, at work and through hobbies and volunteering.
- Transferable skills are valued by employers and should be developed.
- By identifying their skills, your teen can put a plan in place to develop their skills and discover new ones.
- If your teen aims for a career which uses the skills they are good at and enjoy, they are more likely to be happy.

❖

MY CAREER

Caitlin O'Connor
Managing Director, Accelerating Performance
www.acceleratingperformance.ie

Caitlin is a leading expert and consultant in networking, lead generation and marketing strategy. Her clients include many blue chip companies and business organisations. Caitlin is a regular media contributor and university lecturer.

'Start – just start. Don't wait for it to be right.'

How did your career in training begin?

Ironically, I always wanted to be a primary school teacher but I didn't get a place in St Patrick's College due to tough competition, so I did a business course instead and got into Aer Lingus. There, I qualified with a master's in Marketing; and as part of my job in the marketing department, I trained many staff in various sales skills as I was the Focus on Sales award champion. As a marketing professional, the education of call centre staff, suppliers and resellers was continuous. Subconsciously, I was always training and I loved marketing. I often thought what a blessing it was that I didn't get into teaching.

After Aer Lingus, I joined a telecommunications company (ESAT Telecom) and continued with my marketing learning and expertise. I was responsible for all commercial operations, which meant that I had a large team to motivate and train to ensure that results were delivered.

In 2005, I set up my own business in coaching and leadership and I was immediately approached by the Irish Business and Employers Confederation (IBEC) to write a course in networking, which I did. Also, in order to avail of FÁS funding I needed a training qualification. I undertook that and now, nine years on, my business is 75 per cent training and mentoring and 25 per cent consultancy!

What do you enjoy most about what you do now?

I do what I do because it suits my lifestyle. I love to see people grow and become enthused about their futures; I love to see the light bulb go on and the enjoyment that people take from the training. I also love to see companies increase their profits and gain more loyal and excited customers – that's on the consultancy end of things. I love to see people connect and help each other.

What is the toughest thing about your job?
- How some professionals don't value women and the value they bring to a team and to the boardroom. Women bring empathy to a situation, which adds value and balance.
- Being self-employed means balancing prospecting with delivery.
- Promises that are empty!

What motivates you?
Being successful and bringing in new clients. People motivate me – I love people.

Who or what inspired you along the way?
Denis O'Brien – I worked for him for five years. He was amazing – very tough but great fun, empowering and innovative. I made amazing friends working for him, too, who are friends for life. My parents also motivated me and I believe that the greatest motivators are your parents. They were encouraging and always pushed me a little outside my comfort zone. That guaranteed ongoing learning. I will always remember what my Dad said to me the day I resigned from Aer Lingus – a pensionable, semi-state job – 'If you don't take risks you don't make anything.' Those words had a lasting impression!

What advice would you give young people who want a career in the same field?
Start – just start. Don't wait for it to be right.

What has been the biggest lesson in your career to date?
How companies with values not aligned to yours can be the most challenging places to work. Choose a company that has the same values as you have. This means interviewing them

and doing your research as much as them interviewing you. Not all cultures suit everybody. In the early days of one's career, work for a large organisation that follows processes and has structure. This, coupled with a good mentor, will stand you in good stead for life!

❖

STEP 4

Look at their Values: What Matters Most to Them?

It's not hard to make decisions when you know what your values are.

ROY DISNEY

Your teen has talents, passions, strengths and skills. However, one of the most important questions is: What do they want to accomplish with all their talents and skills? What values do they wish to serve? This section focuses on tools that will help you have a conversation around the values that are important to your teen. **Values** are those things that matter to us most and that give us meaning and purpose. They could be health, happiness, love, friendship or wealth. Most successful people choose career paths that express their highest values, the ideals that fulfil their life **purpose**.

We fulfil our purpose when we give what we are here on earth to give and don't leave 'the song inside us unsung'. It is up to every individual to decide for himself or herself what their life purpose is, but often it is connected to what they do for a living. In my own case, I feel the need to write and give inspiration and hope to others. If I came to the end of my life without doing that, I would feel that I had never fulfilled my purpose.

It is important to look within ourselves and examine whether the way we live and work expresses our values, motivations, needs and purpose. Your child will be most successful if their course choice and career choice are in line with their values.

In Step 4, you as a parent will:

- Learn to raise your child's awareness of their values or what matters most to them
- Develop questions and have conversations around values that will uncover your teen's purpose
- Be asked to reflect on your own family values and the values that shaped you and your career choices.

Reflect

Before you look at values with your teenager, consider and reflect on your own values. You could ask the following questions of yourself and consider at the same time what values are core to your family.

Here are some questions for your teenagers to ask themselves in order to define their values and purpose:

- At the end of my life, what do I want to have accomplished or to be remembered for?
- Is there a problem I wish to solve?
- Is there a cause I wish to serve?
- What gives me fire in my belly or gives me energy?
- When do I feel I am in my element?
- What concerns me? (E.g. the environment, entertainment, creative expression, innovation, mind, body, helping others, materialism, learning, spirituality, etc.)
- If I only had six months left to live, how would I choose to spend it?

- If a steel plank were placed between two tall buildings, what would I be prepared to walk the plank for? (E.g. money, family, fame, love, a cause, my community, etc.)

Here is a list of values, but it's not exhaustive. With your teenager, identify and circle which values are most important to them. Can they add any more that aren't on the list?

VALUES LIST

Achievement	Democracy	Imagination	Recognition
Adventure	Discipline	Independence	Responsibility
Balance	Economic security	Justice	Risk-taking
Collaboration	Education	Loyalty	Stability
Community	Equality	Morality	Success
Competition	Excellence	Organisation	Tolerance
Control	Fairness	Peace	Tradition
Co-operation	Freedom	Personal development	Variety
Creativity	Health	Power	Wealth

Below are some of the values and purposes that I have encountered in young people:
- 'I am going to contribute to the safety of my country by joining the Gardaí.'
- 'In my life, I am committed to helping young, vulnerable children at risk.'
- 'My purpose is to create exciting computer games.'
- 'My life will be about making quality breads and pastries for people to enjoy.'

- 'My life motivation is to be the most inspiring history teacher and to make history an interesting subject for young people.'
- 'My life will be about bringing laughter and joy into the world as a comedian.'
- 'My intention is to protect people from fire, injury and risk, as a fireman.'
- 'I intend to make my life about innovation and creating opportunities in the world of business.'

When these young people articulated their values and were able to say what mattered most to them, and then matched their values to a career/occupation, they were able to identify the necessary steps to achieve their purpose. I realise that many young people may not be aware yet of what matters most to them – their personalities and identities are still forming; but try to get them to start noticing when activities or projects come easily and effortlessly to them. Praise your teenager when they do well. The chances are that these achievements encapsulate the values your teenager holds dear.

In addition, you could emphasise the values that your family holds dear and tell stories that demonstrate the values and experiences of grandparents or others who have gone before. I am always struck when looking at the values of students that their main values are love and appreciation for their own immediate family and for their grandparents.

While it is useful to emphasise family values, it is also important that they do not overshadow your child. Some families over-emphasise certain values and this can be passed on from generation to generation. For example, some families may over-stress the importance of security in the form of a permanent, pensionable job. They may push their children towards sectors such as the civil service, in the process allowing their children to pass up other opportunities. Other families may only value work on the land or work that is practical. A teenager who has a keen interest in subjects other than practical ones can feel very lost in this situation.

The poet Patrick Kavanagh expressed this wonderfully in his poem *Stony Grey Soil* when he referred to the land as stealing his youth and 'throwing a ditch' on his vision:

> You flung a ditch on my vision
> Of beauty, love and truth.
> O stony grey soil of Monaghan
> You burgled my bank of youth!

Some young people choose a career in order to please their parents and to satisfy their parents' desire for security, safety and professional status. Parents would naturally prefer to be reassured that their children are secure as adults, but in the long term, giving up happiness for the sake of security is not a good plan. It is possible to be both happy and secure.

Children need to stay true to their *own* values and what matters most to them. Having a purpose and meaning in life, committing to something greater than oneself, can lead to great satisfaction and a sense of wellbeing.

Step 4 Key Points
- Your values have an influence on your career choices.
- You are more likely to be happy in a career that is aligned with your values.
- It is important for your teenager to identify their values so that they can make appropriate career choices.
- The values of parents and families influence teenagers, and while these values may be good, your teen should also be allowed to have their own values.

❖

MY CAREER

Donagh Kelly
Group CEO, KN Network Services
www.knnetworkservices.com

KN Network Services (KNNS) are providers to the telecommunications, civil engineering, rail, electricity and energy sectors in Ireland, the UK and internationally.

'If you want it, go get it yourself – nobody owes you anything!'

How did your career in broadband/telecommunications begin?
During my final years in college, I worked part time with a telecommunications contractor, which naturally gave me exposure to this area and moulded my future.

Did you always want to do what you do now?
I don't think the majority of people can map out their future, as it is difficult to make decisions without all the knowledge you gain with time and experience. I always believed in myself and never doubted my ability in leadership and management, but I did not have a clear career path figured out.

What do you enjoy most about what you do now?
Achieving success in continuing to grow our business across the globe. Seeing our business grow from €10 million per annum to €150 million plus. Our revised annual targets by 2017 are €200 million plus.

What is the toughest thing about your job?

Managing people and the intricacies of human behaviours. Managing personal expectations and demands, which seldom align with the required outputs to justify such demands, is challenging. Management of a business should be based on what the business requires and not what the individual requires. Decisions are sometimes made around people and not around what is actually required. Seeing through this is important.

What motivates you?

Continued success and achievement. If you don't stretch your goals and targets, you can only go one way and that is backwards. We all need challenges in order to stretch, learn and overcome. This breeds enthusiasm and belief in our ability to do more and more. Money is not a motivation in any of my goals – I have enough, I don't need more money. Leading a team across the globe and delivering successful projects gives me a huge amount of pride in what has been achieved and how far we have come.

Who or what inspired you along the way?

I recognise and admire many people in business and what some have achieved is remarkable, but I don't model or copy anyone in particular. I think my parents set the initial mould with both enterprise and education being a foundation stone in our home, coupled with hard work as an everyday ethic. The company you keep also helps create your expectations and forms a sounding board for ideas and proposals. Competition with our peers drives us also.

My wife has always supported me and never questioned or restricted me in any way through all the decisions I have made, which is critical for any entrepreneur. You need to take risks and there are consequences when it goes wrong, so it requires balls and support in order to make difficult decisions.

What advice on getting started would you give young people who want a career in the same field?
Put in the effort and push yourself forward. Remember, you definitely don't know everything and you will make mistakes and that's how you learn. Opportunity doesn't come looking for you, you must find it; if you restrict your options in looking for opportunity it will be harder to realise your ambition. Step out of your comfort zone; the rewards in doing so are massive in all senses.

What has been the biggest lesson in your career to date?
Don't make decisions on a person's ability too early. Give them sufficient time to demonstrate their capabilities and make your own assessment. Base your decisions on fact, not abstract terms. Invest in people and help them to stretch and flourish. If a person does not have the required skill for a function you want performed, teach them quickly or get someone who does, but don't expect a result if you don't change something.

If you had a motto, what would it be?
If you want it, go get it yourself – nobody owes you anything!

What advice would you give your 16-year-old self?
Don't fret if you don't know what you want to do at this stage, but give yourself every chance by getting an education, as it is your initial currency in a career. Your currency is valued in knowledge and experience and the more you have of both, the more valuable you are to both yourself and any employer.

❖

STEP 5

Look at Personality

I want freedom for the full expression of my personality.
MAHATMA GANDHI

We have already looked at **values** and **skills**. Now we are going to look at **personality**. Learning what personality type you have is a valuable way to identify what kind of work will bring you satisfaction. Personality refers to the patterns of behaviour, thought and feelings that influence a person's adjustment to an environment. Simply put, personality refers to the way a person is. Common terms to describe someone include shy, outgoing, reserved, flamboyant, cautious and so on. You might have noticed that your child gets their energy from inside themselves (internally), while other children get their energy from outside themselves (externally), or vice versa. **Extroverts** get their energy from being with other people. **Introverts** gain most of their energy by being away from others and by having enough time to spend alone. No one is entirely an extrovert or an introvert; most people are a mix of both, and children are the same – they might enjoy spending time alone in their room or pottering about in the garage *and* spending time out and about mixing with others. In relation to careers and thinking about the future, extroverts will process their thoughts externally and need time to talk out loud about their ideas in order to be sure about what they really want to do. They will like to toss ideas around. As a parent – and particularly if you are an introvert – you need the patience to step back and let your child ramble. Equally, patience is required for

71

introverts, as they need lots of time and space to process ideas before they are ready to talk. Ask them open-ended questions (see Step 1 on communication) and wait for the answer; it may take them time to consider their response.

Personality can influence career choice, so it is important that your teen chooses a job or path that suits them. Even though there is no straightforward correlation between personality and the fields of work your teen might enjoy, personality still serves as a signpost.

Some teens will be happy in the background, operating machinery, doing mechanics, working in a laboratory; others may want to be in the foreground, out with the public, in the limelight, working in media, working closely with people as a hairdresser, beautician, teacher or solicitor.

Other children may like a mixture of time in the foreground and the background and they may feel more energised by a mix of both. There is a relationship between the people you like to be surrounded by and your skills and values. Giving some time to considering what kind of people they like to be surrounded by and interact with can help your teen make better, more informed career choices.

Step 5 will:

- Introduce the concept of personality and its relation to work
- Offer you a framework to explore your own personality in relation to work
- Give you tools to use with your teen to help them know themselves better
- Enable you to discuss the types of work environment that match your teen's personality.

In terms of personality and occupational choice, teenagers and young adults (between the ages of 15 and 24) go through what career theorist Donald Super calls the exploration stage. During this period, they are finding out who they are, experimenting with careers and forming an individual identity. One way for teenagers to gather information about themselves is through formal tests and self-assessment. Your teen may have completed some tests at school. Very often, young people find it hard to recognise their own personalities, so these tests can be useful. Free tests of this type can be found on the excellent Irish student careers website www.careersportal.ie. Tests can also be administered by qualified guidance counsellors in schools.

Six Types of People

I struggled for years to discover what it was that I wanted to do. When I was 29, I took a 'self-directed search' test designed by Dr John Holland. This test was based on the theory that most people can be categorised into one of six personality types: *Realistic, Investigative, Artistic, Social, Enterprising and Conventional.* The person's top three personality scores are then examined along with the careers that correspond to these personalities. My top three scores pointed to my personality being first *Social,* then *Artistic* and finally *Enterprising.* I remember feeling so relieved and excited that I finally understood my preferences and their corresponding educational, therapeutic and helping careers. The table below outlines in more detail the six personality types that Dr Holland identified.

SIX TYPES OF PEOPLE

R	Realistic	The 'R' type likes practical and realistic jobs. They enjoy working outdoors, working with animals and working with machines and tools. They are often athletic. This type often has stronger mechanical skills than social skills. Sample careers include mechanic, farmer, electrician and surveyor.

I	Investigative	The 'I' type likes to solve problems. They like to know how and why things work. They like to analyse and investigate. Usually they are good at maths and science but often shy away from leadership. This type may like jobs such as biologist, chemist, physicist and medical technologist.
A	Artistic	The 'A' type likes artistic jobs such as artist, singer, dancer, musician, actor/actress etc. They are creative, innovative and have a good imagination. The 'A' type prefers to work with ideas and people rather than doing clerical and administrative tasks.
S	Social	The 'S' type likes to work with and be around people. They like to help others and are interested in how people relate to each other. The 'S' type tends to be helpful, friendly and patient. They like to teach, help or serve others and can lack realistic and mechanical abilities.
E	Enterprising	The 'E' type likes to work with ideas and people rather than things. Careers such as salesperson manager, TV producer, business manager and buyer may appeal to this type. They tend to have good leadership and speaking abilities. They are often interested in business and politics. The 'E' type likes to influence others, to start up projects and to persuade people. They are usually self-confident, ambitious and have leadership abilities, but they may lack scientific ability.

C	**Conventional**	The 'C' type likes to work indoors and to organise things. They like to work with numbers. Often they are suited to banking, accountancy, being a tax expert or an administrator. They are usually practical, efficient, careful and persistent. C people like detailed work and like to complete tasks and projects. Sometimes they can lack artistic skills.

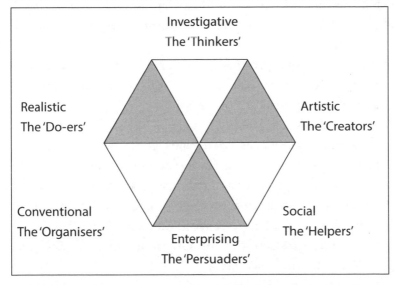

TASK C: WHAT TYPES OF PERSONALITY HAS YOUR TEEN?

Ask your child to figure out which of these categories most suits them and/or which of the six types of people they would prefer to hang out with, work with or be surrounded by. It is important when using personality tests not to feel pigeonholed by a type or label. Brainstorm the occupations related to these areas and/or take John Holland's online test at www.self-directed-search.com.

Out of curiosity, you and your partner could each do this test for yourselves and see how near or far your current job or life is from your personality type.

Exploring areas of ability, interests, skills, values and personality provides a snapshot of the present in relation to your child's future and aids them in making good career choices. These are, however, useful indicators or signposts only in terms of the 'bigger picture', which is dealt with in the next section, which looks at dreams and ideal outcomes. Refer to the 'Knowing Yourself' section under Further Resources for tips on how to gain a deeper level of self-knowledge.

When looking at personality, it is important to acknowledge the concept of 'emotional intelligence' or EI. Emotional intelligence refers to an understanding of the human mind. Daniel Goleman, in his article 'What Makes a Leader?' (*Best of Harvard Business Review*, 1998) describes emotional intelligence as being self-aware, which means: knowing your own emotions; being able to self-regulate or manage your emotions; having social skills (handling relationships); having empathy (recognising emotion in others); and being able to motivate yourself. Emotional intelligence is an important part of any personality test as it measures how one copes with stress and change in life.

Connected to emotional intelligence is Howard Gardner's theory of multiple intelligences. This is another indicator of your teenager's preferred way of being in the world. As a parent, it can add to your understanding of how they see the world.

Multiple Intelligences

As well as having different skills, each of us is intelligent in different ways. It is useful to know which intelligences we have developed and which we still could develop. In his book *Frames of Mind*, Howard Gardner identified seven kinds of intelligence. There are typical roles and careers associated with each intelligence. Below is an overview of Gardner's multiple intelligences and examples of careers that often correspond to those intelligences.

MULTIPLE INTELLIGENCES

Intelligence	Characteristics	Suitable careers
Linguistic intelligence	Being good with words, writing, speaking, explaining ideas, learning languages	Journalism, law, training, teaching, linguistics, translating, media consultancy, TV and radio presentation
Logical/ mathematical intelligence	Being good with numbers, solving problems and sorting out facts and figures, analysing and interpreting data	Science, engineering, computing, accountancy, banking, insurance, being an actuary and careers involving mathematics
Musical intelligence	Having an awareness and appreciation of sound and rhythm, an ability to sing and/or play a musical instrument and understanding the relationship between sound and feeling	Musician, music producing, sound engineering, piano tuning, voice coaching, DJing, teaching music, providing voice-overs
Kinaesthetic/ body intelligence	Involves skilful body movement, manual dexterity, balance, eye and body co-ordination and being good with your hands	Dancing, athletics, acting, sports instruction, the fire brigade, commercial fishing, driving, craft, cheffing, gardening, the army and paramedicine

Social/ interpersonal intelligence	Perception of other people's feelings, an ability to mix and relate well to others, negotiation skills, co-operation skills and an understanding of relationships	Counselling, human resources, psychology, occupational therapy, teaching, medicine, advertising, coaching, travel organising, media consultancy
Intrapersonal/ intuitive intelligence	High level of self-awareness, being able to understand one's own thoughts, feelings and behaviours, understanding the relationship between self and others	Therapy, spiritual ministry, theology, law, art
Naturalist intelligence	Ability to relate to natural surroundings and the environment, being able to relate to and handle animals, work with marine life, the earth or plant life	Farming, agriculture, horticulture, marine science, fishing, landscape architecture, wildlife ranger, food science and environmental research

For a test on multiple intelligences, please see Further Resources, page 206.

VARK Learning Styles

This is an even simpler version of the multiple intelligences idea. Developed by educationalist Neil Fleming, VARK analyses people's preferred ways of learning and developing. Some of us learn best by seeing things (pictures, graphs, etc.), some of us by listening, some by reading and writing and some by experiencing. The acronym VARK stands for visual, aural, read/write and kinaesthetic, and these are sensory modalities that are employed in learning. All of us can be 'multi-modal' in our learning styles. Knowing their learning styles can help your teen in their studies, as well as their motivation and overall performance. See www.vark-learn.com for a free online VARK questionnaire to find out what your learning style is.

- **Visual (V):** People are 'visual' if they learn best by watching or reading instructions in the form of charts, graphics, spider diagrams, films/videos or PowerPoint presentations.
- **Aural/auditory (A):** If you prefer to hear information, you may be 'aural'; in other words, you like to learn by listening or repeating information aloud. Lectures, group discussions, radio, debates, online discussions or podcasts can best assist this style of learning.
- **Read/write (R):** This is all about a preference for learning information that is displayed as words. Lists, the internet, diaries, dictionaries, books and manuals can best assist learning. Note-taking and creating lists of words also helps if this is your learning style.
- **Kinaesthetic (K):** If you learn best by trying things out for yourself, you may have a 'kinaesthetic' learning style. This means that you learn best by experiencing things, carrying out a task – either simulated or real. For those who are predominantly kinaesthetic, it is essential that learning is connected to the real world and that it is concrete and practical. Learning in a way that involves either movement or using objects that can be held, grasped, tasted or felt will accelerate the learning outcomes.

Apart from home economics, art, PE, technical graphics, construction studies and woodwork, most subjects at school don't include kinaesthetic learning techniques. I find that many kinaesthetic learners are frustrated both in school and in the workplace, if they cannot move around or have a job where they are active and physically involved. Identifying kinaesthetic learning preferences can relieve many learning frustrations. It is important to keep this in mind for study and for career choices.

Bear in mind when exploring these tests that we are all a mixture of styles and preferences and that none of us falls into one category alone.

Let's recap!

After using the techniques and tips outlined above, can your teen answer the following questions?

- What are my **strengths**?
- What are my **skills**?
- What are my **values**?
- What **personality type** do I have?
- What are my main **intelligences** (in what ways am I intelligent)?
- What are my **learning styles**?

Step 5 Key Points

- Your personality is vital to what type of work you will be happy doing. We may be extroverts, introverts or a mixture of both.
- People's personalities can be broadly classed as: Realistic, Investigative, Social, Enterprising or Conventional.
- We are usually a combination of these, although one type might predominate.
- Which personality type do you think you are? In light of this, consider how your career choices have suited your personality.
- Get your teen to take the online personality test and brainstorm occupations that might suit their personality.
- Encourage your teen to examine in what way they are intelligent using a multiple intelligences test or by looking at the different categories of intelligence.

- Have your teen look at VARK to determine their learning styles; this may help their motivation both in study now, and in their future performance in the workplace.
- In order for your teen to make informed, appropriate career choices, they need to be aware of their strengths, skills, values and personality.

MY CAREER

Lieutenant Sinead Hunt
Irish Defence Forces
www.military.ie

The Army is the largest component of the Defence Forces, which recruits on three levels: for cadets, recruits and apprentices. Other sectors of the Defence Forces are the Air Corps and the Naval Service.

'There is something to be learned from every job you do ... always take something from it and bring it to the next challenge you face.'

How did your career in the Defence Forces begin?
I started with Officer Cadet Training in the Military College, Defence Forces Training Centre. This is a 15-month training programme, which covers many fields of study – both tactical and academic in nature – in order to prepare students morally, mentally and physically for their role as leaders in the Defence Forces.

Did you always want to do what you do now?
As my Dad and Granddad both served in the Irish Defence
Forces there has always been a strong military influence in
my family. I didn't expect to follow suit initially, despite
being somewhat exposed to military values and conduct from
an early age. It wasn't the obvious choice while attending
an all girls' secondary school. I enjoy design and analytical
problem-solving, so I chose to study mechanical engineering
in college. This was a great foundation course and opened up
many options. On completion of this, as a career the Defence
Forces appealed to me as there are opportunities to branch
into specialised technical appointments such as Engineering,
Ordnance and IT. This offers the unique opportunity to
balance the desk job with working outdoors in a physically
demanding environment as part of a team.

What do you enjoy most about what you do now?
The variety and challenge. One week you can find yourself
living in a hole in the ground and skinning rabbits to cook
(survival training) and the next week you're outside Áras an
Uachtaráin in your shiniest uniform presenting your troops for
inspection on a Presidential Guard of Honour – and that's only
a taste of the variety of tasks! I have just completed a placement
working in Human Resources. It was very exciting to be
involved in the recruitment campaign for both general service
recruits and officer cadets. Now that these new recruits and
cadets have commenced training, I have returned to my unit
in the Cavalry Corps and expect to conduct courses in the areas
of reconnaissance and armoured vehicle and gunnery training.

What is the toughest thing about your job?
For me, it's having to spend long periods of time away from

family and friends, although you do make close bonds with your classmates and colleagues while working and living together. There is a strong underlying support system unlike any other workforce that I've been a part of and that helps make things easier.

What motivates you?
A career in the Defence Forces is very challenging – both mentally and physically – and there are times, particularly in training, when it pushes you beyond the limits of what you think you are capable of. Coming out on the other side of that is very rewarding. When I experience this, I find it is strong motivation to persevere the next time I'm challenged, as who knows the limits of what we can accomplish?

Who or what inspired you along the way?
My parents are a huge inspiration to me. Between Dad serving overseas with the United Nations on peace-keeping missions to Lebanon, Bosnia and Liberia and Mam working transatlantic shifts as a cabin crew manager with Aer Lingus, it baffles me to think how they managed to balance it all! I also find that listening to those working with you and relating their experience to the task at hand provides valuable advice and inspiration.

What advice on getting started would you give young people who want a career in the same field?
Read up about the job on our website, www.military.ie, initially to identify what area of the Defence Forces interests you. Then begin to develop the relevant skills, such as teamwork, motivation, physical fitness, leadership, problem-solving and decision-making in your everyday life through school, sports,

clubs or other hobbies. The Reserve Defence Forces is a great opportunity to experience a career in the Defence Forces on a part-time basis.

What has been the biggest lesson in your career to date?
That there is something to be learned from every job you do. No matter how big, small, irrelevant or badly you think it might have worked out, always take something from it and bring it to the next challenge you face.

If you had a motto, what would it be?
I don't go by a personal motto but the motto of my unit, the First Armoured Cavalry Squadron, is: 'Through the mud and the blood to the green fields beyond.'

What advice would you give to your 16-year-old self?
Keep striving for what you want and you will get there one way or another; when one door closes another one opens. Also, make sure you get enjoyment out of getting there, to ensure it's really what you want!

❖

STEP 6

Encouraging Dreams

If you can dream it you can do it. If you can't imagine it, then it is genuinely impossible.

WALT DISNEY

This section helps you look at dreams and aid your teen in finding their 'mission' and 'purpose' in life. Identifying a mission or purpose in life helps your teen avoid a dead end job where they live for Fridays and are bored out of their minds. Having dreams and a vision helps your teen feel alive and focused on making a meaningful contribution to the world.

Dreams can be fragile. When we're young, we often know what we want to do with our lives, but sometimes we talk ourselves out of our dreams or let other people dissuade us. Perhaps we do not pursue our dreams because we feel we are not clever enough, or that they are not in keeping with family wishes. We may feel that our peers or community will reject us if we break the mould and follow our calling. Even if we don't follow our dreams, they will still be there when we are adults, but they will lie dormant until we activate them.

Step 6:
- Introduces the importance of having our own dreams
- Looks at the influence parents can have on teenagers' dreams
- Gives you tools to have conversations with your teenager about their ideal future
- Gives you a platform to discuss the qualities of the people your teen finds inspirational

- Acknowledges the influence that mental images/self-concepts can have on our dreams
- Encourages you to help your teen create positive mental images
- Stresses the importance of continuing to grow and reach beyond our comfort zones.

On countless occasions, I have met adults who speak of childhood dreams, of becoming primary teachers, midwives, engineers, architects, artists and so on. During coaching sessions many people in their mid-thirties and forties talk about their dreams to connect with children, deliver babies, create art, write poetry or create something lasting like a bridge or a building. A renewed energy, pride, confidence and personal satisfaction returns to their lives when they revisit and pursue their original life dreams. Revisiting life dreams can require a lot of change and upheaval but, ultimately, it leads to a contented and rich life. The psychologist Carl Jung wrote that 'the greatest damage to the child is the *unlived* life of the parents'. All too often, we place our own unfulfilled dreams upon our children.

In my own case, I would love to have learned to play the violin; however, I lacked the necessary focus and discipline. It is entirely possible that I could transfer my unfulfilled dream to my child and push them to learn the violin.

Sometimes, parents who did not go to college or parents who struggle to get steady work can overvalue education and place too much pressure on their children to achieve. They want their children to have the best options possible. It is useful to step back and examine our own motivations and our desires for our children. How much of it is actually in their interest and how much of it is us transferring our dreams to them?

> Living out our dreams is not a selfish act, but rather a gift to our families and those around us.

Reflect

Before we move on to your teenager, please think about the following questions:

- What dreams did you have as a teenager that you let go of?
- What talents have you still to express in your life?
- How close or far away are you today from living your dreams?

Examining your own dreams is time well spent and it puts you in a better position to help your teenager connect with their dreams, speak about them and make them come true. I have seen many teenagers unable to focus or study because they didn't know what they were going to do with their lives or what direction to go in. Helping your teenager clarify their future dream gives their learning more meaning in relation to their overall plan. In my experience, dreams can provide the 'light bulb' moment for a teenager to engage with school.

I once had a student who wasn't engaged in her learning and whose head was forever in 'chick-lit' books. Her mind was lost in the fantasy world of teenage romantic novels. We chatted and discovered that her dream was to travel and work on ships as a marine engineer. When she really connected with the excitement and thrill she would experience if she someday travelled and worked on the ships, she made a decision to study. She gave her Mum the 'chick-lit' book she was reading at the time, didn't look back and really concentrated on her studies.

Her mum told me that she took the book back after her exams. She now works on ships in the Atlantic and feels fully alive.

Remember that life is a journey. Knowing your destination or dream vision makes it easier to take action and progress in the right direction rather than go round in circles.

TASK D: DESCRIBING THEIR IDEAL FUTURE LIFE

Ask your child to describe their ideal life in the future without the constraints of time, money or ability. Ask them:

- What do they see in their dream future?
- What are they doing?
- What are other people saying when they have their ideal future?
- What will I hear you saying when you have got it?
- What will I see you doing when you have got it?
- What will you gain when you have got it?
- What will you lose?
- Is it worth the cost to you?

Jot down the answers on a piece of paper and you will have an overall vision that you can both plan towards. Tell them that they can achieve what they want, even if it seems far-fetched. Keep in mind the words of Goethe:

Treat people as they are, and they remain that way.
Treat them as though they were what they can be,
and we help them become what they are capable of becoming.

TASK E: CAREER DREAM COLLAGE

Create a **career dream collage**. Get your child to look at all the people they know – family, friends, people in the community, people on TV and in the movies, pop stars, etc. If they are attracted to somebody get them to write down their name or cut out a picture of them and discuss what it is about their skills or personality that they admire. They can write the words down or draw their ideas beside the person's picture. You could use the following questions to stimulate the thought process:

- Who are the people around you who have careers that interest you?
- What is it about their attitude or behaviour that you admire?
- What is it about them that you consider special?
- What part of their purpose, personal aspirations, drive, focus or lifestyle would you like to have?
- Which of their qualities do you already have?

It is rare for a teenager to be 100 per cent in awe of any one person, but by taking the best of everyone around them and putting these bits together, they are creating a jigsaw of their life dream. They can expand the collage by doing internet research on the person they admire or by speaking to someone in the family or community they look up to.

Finally, ask them if they were to take all the bits of qualities, skills and mindsets of the people in the collage and put it inside themselves, what would it be like? Have a conversation and draw or write it out on a piece of paper. Encourage them to imitate the positive habits, mindsets and qualities of those they wish to copy.

Hollie's Career Dream Collage

Here are Hollie's answers to questions about her dream collage.

Who are the people who have careers that interest you?
Roger Federer, Queen, Lang Lang, Adele, Hozier.

What is it about their attitude or behaviour that you admire?
What is it about them that you consider special?
Roger Federer's great style of play: he's top of his game.
Queen – great performers, unique, flashy and entertaining.
Lang Lang – gifted piano player, young, open, teaching great workshops and in his 20s.
Adele – has her own sense of fashion, she is genuine, down to earth, writes her own songs and is personal.

What part of their purpose, personal aspirations, drive, focus or lifestyle would you like to have?
They have good personalities and know themselves. They are rich and secure and can go shopping. I would like to have many choices in life and not to feel restricted. They have accomplished a lot and are interested in continuous improvement. In life, they are making a difference and inspiring people. Their gifts touch others.

Which of their qualities do you already have?
When I want something, I work for it. I have the motivation and desire. Anything I set my mind to I give it a hundred per cent.

Finally, if you were to take all these bits of qualities, skills, and mindsets of the people in the collage and put it inside yourself, what would it be like?
I would be focused and dedicated on one or two things. I would

be very confident, know my own mind, and make my own unique brand. I would be motivated and able to plan my time and deal with a hectic schedule.

I did this exercise with a group of teenagers and they gained great clarity about what they wanted in the future. One particular boy included race horses, the army, travel, money, happiness, his own family and a house for the future. Others got excited about the work they could be doing, many of them choosing the helping professions, such as the fire service, teaching, social care and physiotherapy. It helped them focus on the overall lifestyle they wanted and what it would take to realise it.

Visualisation

George Bernard Shaw said, 'imagination is the beginning of creation. You imagine what you desire, you will what you imagine, and at last you create what you will.' When teenagers come to me and tell me their dreams for the future, sometimes they fear that their dreams are not achievable. I ask them to visualise their ideal future before sleeping at night, and to include as much detail as possible, to include the desired environment, activity, people and achievements, and to feel the emotions associated with this scene.

A 17-year-old girl once came to me who was frustrated with learning and school. She found it really hard to concentrate and wanted to drop out before her final exams. Her head was full of worries and images of failure. When we looked at what she really wanted in life she told me that, more than anything, she wanted to be an air steward. She really felt that this was an impossible dream given her struggle with learning. I suggested that before sleeping at night she should focus on relaxing and seeing herself on a movie screen achieving success as an air steward; that she should picture herself in her uniform on planes serving passengers and travelling all over the world. After some time her confidence was built up again and she was able to connect being at school with her end goal of being an air steward.

Pictures of Ourselves

The following quote from Gloria Steinem says it all:

> Without leaps of imagination, or dreaming, we lose the excitement of possibilities. Dreaming, after all, is a form of planning.

Unless we can dream and use our imagination, we can become flat and get stuck in a rut. Dreaming allows us to plan towards the future. In his book *Psycho-Cybernetics* Maxwell Maltz explains that the power of the imagination can be used to achieve great results. He states that a person's current self-image – the way they see themselves – is built upon their own imagined pictures of themselves in the past, which grew out of evaluations that they made about past experiences. For example, I have a very clear picture of myself at the age of five unable to do the sum 5 + 8. I was scared of the teacher and felt under pressure to find the answer with her leaning over me. So from that day on I decided that I was the kind of person who couldn't do maths and, as a result, my brain was never willing to give maths a chance! Our self-image is constructed out of our own belief that 'This is the sort of person I am.'

Motivational speaker and author Wayne Dyer says that motivating children to have greater aspirations in life is essentially the task of working on their pictures of themselves in all areas of their lives. If a teenager has a strong self-image or picture of themselves, they are more likely to be confident and centred enough not to be swayed or toppled by the opinions others have of them.

You can help 'rewire' your teen's imagination to create an even healthier self-image. When they repeatedly visualise themselves acting and feeling differently, these positive images are imprinted on the brain and nervous system. Soon change becomes automatic. Your language and comments can help this process, as outlined below.

Negative comment	Positive comment
The sea is a dangerous place.	I'm hearing that you think the sea is dangerous, but give swimming lessons a go. It'll be great fun!
No one in our family has a business head.	I'm hearing that you think no one in the family is good at business. That shouldn't stop *you*. Try out your idea and give it go. It has great potential!

As in the examples above, first acknowledge your teen's fear/ worry; show that you have been listening at a deep level. (Of course, sometimes fear and anxiety has its uses – it can serve as a self-protection mechanism. When teens are fearless they can be too daring and that has consequences too.) Then mention past strengths and encourage them to change the negative images in their head into positive ones.

Here are more examples of how your teen's inner pictures could be rewired:

Teen	Parent
I'll never do well in my exams.	I'm hearing that you don't feel confident, but you will do well. Before you go to sleep, just picture yourself getting the grades you want and hold on to the feeling it gives you.
I am afraid of not making any new friends in college.	I'm hearing that you are afraid you won't be able to mix with new people. You know that you make friends easily in new environments. I can see that you will make lots of friends in college too.
What if I don't get a part-time job?	I'm hearing that getting work is important to you. You're really good at asking for work and you have lots of good contacts. See yourself in a part-time job that you like and that pays well.

This method of visualising, rewiring their thoughts and feelings, really works with teenagers and helps alleviate their worries and anxieties about the future. After all, worrying curbs their creativity and thinking capacity. In my work as a guidance counsellor, many students have told me that this technique has helped them relax and feel less worried when they were overwhelmed by the stress of exams and school. It helped them see themselves doing well in exams, getting what they wanted and feeling happy at home, with friends and at school.

Comfort Zones

As a parent you may want to limit your child to safe and familiar dreams; you may want to protect them from dreaming too big. You may even fear that they will fail or be disappointed if they set their sights too high. Adopt the Nike motto – 'Just do it!' – or say, 'Go for it!' Tell them that they can do anything if they put their minds to it and that nothing is impossible. From my experience, there are too many adults walking around with unlived dreams in their hearts. So foster a different reality for your teenager.

A 'comfort zone' is a place where we feel comfortable but where we are not growing or being stretched. For some people a comfort zone might correlate to hanging out with the same people all the time, going to the same shops or cafés or even sitting in the same seat in a staff room or canteen.

The following story by Francis Padinjarakera illustrates the importance of moving beyond our comfort zones.

Treasures

One of the disciples told a sage that contact with him had turned his life upside down. 'I had come to dip my toes in the water but now I am in deep waters.'

'If it is safety you wanted you should have stayed on the shore,' said the sage; 'but the security of the land would have been a prison for your spirit.'

'I see that now. Yet the fear is still there,' conceded the disciple.

'Great treasures are found in the depths of the ocean and my job is to help you take the plunge,' the sage said. 'It's ironic, but your fear is of your own depth and the vastness of the treasures within!' (Francis J. Padinjarekara, *A Dewdrop in the Ocean: Wisdom Stories for Turbulent Times*)

Step 6 Key Points
- It is important for teenagers to have dreams or a vision for life.
- Parents can profoundly influence and shape their children's dreams.
- Examine and become aware of how close or far away you are from living your own dreams.

- Tools such as a dream collage can help your teen gain clarity as to what their dreams are.
- Your teenager's mental images can shape their ability to realise their dreams.
- We can rewire our brains to transform negative images/statements into positive images.
- In order for your teenager to grow and progress towards their dreams it is important that you encourage them to move beyond their comfort zones.

❖

MY CAREER

Ian Power
Executive Director, SpunOut.ie
www.spunout.ie

SpunOut.ie is a not-for-profit website created by young people for young people. It serves young people aged 16–25 in Ireland and Northern Ireland. The service provided by SpunOut promotes wellbeing and healthy living in order to prevent and intervene in harmful behaviour where it occurs in young people.

'Building relationships and influencing others are probably two of the most valuable things you can learn.'

How did your career begin?
I studied Economics and Politics at university because I thought I wanted to be a journalist. After a couple of years

working in various newspapers while I was at college, I realised it wasn't for me and didn't really have a plan when I finished college. I worked in the Students' Union for a year after my degree and it was a great experience – I learned loads of really important life and work skills from that year. Afterwards, I saw an advert for a job working with young people in a school in Hackney in London and I decided to apply. I spent two and a half fantastic years working there with inspirational young people, who – despite all the challenges they faced – decided what they wanted to be in life and worked hard to achieve their goals.

I then came back to Ireland to work in communications for the not-for-profit youth information website SpunOut.ie. I had a bit of experience editing the college paper and magazine and had worked as a journalist, so I had a fair idea of how to do the job but I didn't have any formal training – just lots of practical experience – and I used my cover letter to show what I would do if given the job. After a year, I became the director of SpunOut.ie and I'm really enjoying the challenge of the new role.

Did you always want to do what you do now?
Not at all. I didn't know what I wanted to do. I never had a plan. I took every interesting opportunity that came my way and I never regretted it. I didn't mean to choose to work in the not-for-profit sector, but I'm so glad I'm here because it's somewhere you can have a real impact if you work hard.

I never thought this is where I'd be at this stage in my career but I'm glad I never stressed about my career plan. I just made sure I enjoyed coming to work every day. When you stop enjoying getting up for your job in the morning, that's when it's time to find a new challenge, I think.

What do you enjoy most about what you do now?
I love the organisation I work for. My role is to make sure we are making the biggest impact we can and to ensure that we have enough money to keep our doors open and our website fully stocked with quality youth information content.

I love the new skills I'm learning too – team management, fundraising, finance and accounting, and policy-making. I'm always ready to learn and to think about new ways of doing things – I think that's vital to be able to do your job well. You should always be learning in a job; if you're not, it's time to find a new challenge.

What is the toughest thing about your job?
I think it's the multi-tasking and trying to juggle priorities so none of them ever falls. It's hard to keep the organisation moving in one direction, with a shared vision and focus, but we're very lucky with the team we have and we're definitely seeing the benefits of our efforts.

What motivates you?
I'm motivated to try to make a small difference to the lives of our readers. I got great job satisfaction from working with my students in London because I was able to see them grow into such awesome people over two years. The work I'm doing now is on a macro as opposed to an individual level, but I project that awareness that I developed in London onto the work we do for the hundreds of thousands of young people who visit our website. Finding ways to improve the experience and wellbeing of our readers is what motivates me. I don't think I would have the same motivation if I worked in the corporate world.

Who or what inspired you along the way?
Lots of people inspired me along the way. I had so many great role models in school, at home and in college. The commonality among them was that they all worked hard and I realised hard work will get you wherever you want to go.

What advice on getting started would you give young people who want a career in the same field?
Volunteer. Get out there, help where you can and, most important, learn.

What has been the biggest lesson in your career to date?
The biggest lesson has probably been the importance of networking and being able to build relationships with people. Building relationships and influencing others are probably two of the most valuable things you can learn.

If you had a motto, what would it be?
Work hard, but play hard too. It's so important to have a balance in your life.

What advice would you give your 16-year-old self?
Don't stress. Life is so unpredictable that you can't always legislate for every eventuality. Go with the flow and absorb everything around you.

❖

STEP 7

Motivation and Action!

Vision without action is a dream.
Action without vision is simply passing the time.
Action with vision is making a positive difference.

JOEL BARKER

All dreams require **motivation** and **action** to make them become a reality. I frequently meet teenagers whose main hurdle on the road to success is lack of motivation and, as a consequence, a lack of action. This can be the source of many arguments between parents and teens, leading to tension and stress for all concerned. Step 7 is a key step in helping your teen translate their dreams into reality. Without focusing on motivation, your career conversations so far will not be effective.

Step 7:

- Identifies the importance of motivation
- Asks you to reflect on your own level of motivation in relation to your previous goals and ambitions
- Looks at possible sources of motivation for your teen in the form of activities
- Offers a planning template that helps you and your teen create an action plan to realise their dreams
- Addresses the issue of procrastination and what could get in the way of your teen realising their dreams
- Examines ways to overcome these setbacks
- Points out the value of inspiration in motivating us.

Motivation

In order to turn a dream into reality, **motivation** is required. When it comes to career goals, some teenagers live in a fantasy world. They have a dream, but don't take constructive action or the steps needed to realise their dream. Having a plan, beating procrastination and taking a series of positive, constructive steps all translate into action. Looking at courses, attending college open days, talking to people on courses or in careers of interest, figuring out the points needed and the corresponding amount of study required, enquiring about apprenticeships, getting a sponsor – these are all constructive steps that will lead to results.

People are more motivated to take action when it serves a good greater than themselves. The former Olympic swimmer Adrian Moorhouse, in his book (written with Graham Jones) *Developing Mental Toughness*, expressed this well when he said that people are capable of extraordinary commitment when they adopt the attitude that they have chosen to do a particular thing rather than feeling they have been forced. They believe that their motivation is healthy, because they can rationalise it. Motivation can take two forms: **towards** or **away from**. (This can be expressed in other ways, for example approach or avoidance; inspiration or desperation.)

The first type of motivation moves us towards a set of actions, while the other moves us away from a situation or set of circumstances. For example, a poor school report might motivate us to try harder, or a lack of fitness might motivate us to get fitter. Some teenagers are motivated to do well in school in order to *move away* from their background, buy a house in a safer area and have a life that involves fewer struggles. Others are inspired to take action *towards* making a national sports team, writing music or inventing something for the Young Scientist competition. Studies show that adopting a set of actions *towards* a goal leads to greater persistence and achievement.

When I was 18, I worked in a bar in London. Clocking up long hours in return for little pay motivated me to get a qualification that would lead me to a job with good working conditions. Similarly, a Dublin journalist wrote that after he failed the Leaving Certificate and received a D in English, he found that a job cleaning toilets finally gave him the motivation to better himself and to study for a degree at night. There are many ways to spark motivation and the important thing is to find the way that is right for your child.

Néidín Coulahan's Story

'I was badly bullied in primary school. This experience knocked me back and affected my self-esteem and confidence. In sixth class, I discovered Taekwon-Do (kickboxing) and through martial arts, I found inner strength. Slowly but surely, I gained confidence, realised my own importance, and joined a new social group.

'Taekwon-Do taught me the art of discipline. Participation in the martial arts process helped my motivation at school and in life and gave me a greater sense of balance. My coach didn't take the soft approach. He expected the best from me. Sometimes, I feel that parents can give in too easily to excuses and tiredness. My teachers at school and, in particular, my history teacher supported both my sporting and academic goals.

'When I did my Leaving Cert, I had two major goals. The first was to compete in Taekwon-Do at a world level in Korea. The second was to be a primary school teacher. Every morning, I trained for two hours before going to school. My regime was a strict one. I followed a strict nutritional, training and study plan. After my Leaving Cert exams, I went off to Korea to compete in the World Championship Games and won a bronze medal. I was elated! That same summer my exam results came out and I got 425 points – 50 points short of those needed for primary teaching that

year, so I didn't get a place to do primary teaching. All my life, I had had my heart set on primary teaching, but this setback did not deter me. I had a Plan B and a Plan C. Plan B was to do an arts degree and follow it with a postgraduate qualification in teaching, and Plan C was an access route to college through the Liberties College.

'*In September of that year, 2010, I started an arts degree in St Patrick's College. Now, going to college was a bit daunting as I was surrounded by students whose parents were teachers or who had been to college. As I am from an area that is working class, it is not the norm to go to college. Therefore, I had to have the courage to challenge that norm. Neither of my parents had been to college and my Dad was deaf. Nevertheless, they were very encouraging of me and helped me in a practical way.*

'*I felt that I needed to prove myself to myself while I was at college. I availed of all the supports from the lecturers and from the Access Office. The discipline of Taekwon-Do pushed me to achieve excellence. If my results were not to my satisfaction, I adjusted my daily habits such as eating and sleeping and re-adjusted other behaviours in order to improve my outcomes.*

'*I took a proactive approach in college, as I felt I needed to prove myself in order to break the mould. I established a kickboxing club. In addition, I ran as Women's Officer and took part in the Women for Election campaign. Putting myself forward and out there gave me new skills, a new confidence and a greater edge.*

'*In my summers, I did not lie about. I set up a Taekwon-Do club for children in my local area, because I wanted to give them the gift that I had been given and which had helped my resilience. I volunteered at the local Gaelscoil summer camps and this gave me huge breadth of experience in working with younger children.*

'*Today, I am in teaching practice in a working-class area. I am six months away from achieving my goal of becoming a primary school teacher. My heart is full of joy and satisfaction as I can see the impact I can have on the lives of the children in my class. At school, I see the value of education as it exposes the children to arts, sports, music and drama. They could not afford these activities at home. Education opens up their worlds. I feel that I am a role model to the children as I too am from a working-class background. Often I say to them, "If I can go to college, you can do it too."*

'Based on my journey and my experience, I would say to young people: Stick to what you want to do. Don't worry too much about the CAO points. There are access routes, mature student entry, and many ways around it. Think of different approaches and don't settle for second best.'

Reflect (Time for You)

Think back to some of the goals and ambitions you achieved in the past. They might be losing weight, passing exams, getting a job, improving your fitness, starting a company ...

- What sorts of key techniques did you use?
- What approach worked for you?
- How did you plan step by step?
- Did you reward yourself?
- Did you share your goals with others?
- Did you rely on willpower?
- Did you remind yourself of the benefits of achieving your goals?
- Did you tell yourself of the costs of not achieving your goals?
- What helped you achieve success?

> The best form of motivation is self-motivation and that is a door that can only be unlocked from within.

External motivators – bribes, warnings, sticks and carrots – can inhibit real motivation. Sometimes parents promise a reward such as money, computer games or a trip in exchange for good study habits. On the other hand, threats like removing an Xbox or confiscating a mobile phone if teens don't study or attend school can have a negative effect; some of them will dig their heels in.

Teenagers need to find reasons to study within themselves, independent of rewards or threats. Internal motivation gets young people places and produces results. Therefore, your child will drum up self-motivation based on a challenge, a goal, values and/or a belief that what they are doing has relevance in their lives.

> You can motivate by fear and you can motivate by reward. But both of these methods are only temporary – the only lasting thing is self-motivation. (Homer Rice)

Having looked with your child at their dreams, try to identify goals for their future and seek challenges that relate to those goals. If teenagers do more of the activities that absorb their attention, the more they will learn about where their true motivation lies. These activities might include playing hurling, doing a construction project or a science experiment, participating in speech and drama or playing in a band. The more excitement and enthusiasm they feel for certain activities, the clearer the clues to their future career. You can increase their access to activities that fully engage them where they are in the 'zone' or 'flow'.

Identify when your teen is in the 'zone' or 'flow'. This could manifest as a positive feeling, a picture of success in their heads or words they say to themselves. Get them to relate this feeling to areas where they feel less confident. Encourage them to seek inspiration in books, places, nature, music, sport or people. This will nurture their souls and help them start moving forward.

Lucy's Story

Lucy, a Leaving Cert student, came to me and shared how the book *The Secret* helped motivate her. She applied some of the ideas in the book to her dream of becoming a paediatric nurse. First she created a vision board* containing pictures of her ideal life in the future and placed it above her study desk. Then she posted up the number of points she needed to get into the college course of her choice. She then internalised the wonderful feeling of having already achieved her dream in advance. Lucy went around the school imagining that she was in a hospital ward with children. She brought her purpose to help heal children into every class and made the connections between her study and life purpose. Today, Lucy is a qualified nurse and says she is living out her career dream.

* A vision board is 'a collage of images, pictures and affirmations of your dreams and desires'. See 'How to make a Vision Board', www.wikihow.com/Make-a-Vision-Board.

Teenagers can be put off by subjects that seem to have no relevance to their lives. Therefore, connecting tasks or topics to their own lives, their overall dream, and the points they require for certain courses all help motivation. It is vital that your teenager feeds their well of inspiration continually otherwise they will become bored and complacent.

Carrie's Story

On the surface, Carrie seemed depressed. This 13-year-old girl had been crying for three weeks, practically non-stop. She was advised to come and have a chat and after some time I realised that Carrie was bored and under-stimulated both inside and outside school. Every day was 'Groundhog Day'! We looked at what inspired her and other ways she could tap into inspiration. She was a highly creative girl with an interest in Japanese animation, so to feed her creativity we discussed options such as joining book clubs and writing clubs, visiting museums, going to animation festivals and meeting new people. Soon the sadness lifted as Carrie filled her time with activities that inspired her and set tasks and goals for herself aligned with her interests.

Creating Winning Habits

Professor Richard Wiseman conducted motivation studies on five thousand people and he uncovered four key steps to success:

1. Having the right kind of plan
2. Telling your friends and family
3. Focusing on the benefits
4. Rewarding yourself every step of the way.

(For more information, see Wiseman's book *59 Seconds: Think a Little, Change a Lot.*)

Having the right kind of plan is crucial to your teen achieving their career goals. Once they have identified their goals, they can break them down into sub-goals or manageable 'tortoise' steps. Slow and steady wins the race; allowing yourself to feel overwhelmed by the whole task can make it impossible.

Students who want to study medicine are often put off by the enormous task of passing the Health Professions Admissions Test (HPAT), an aptitude test for medicine, and achieving the high points needed for the courses. Professor Wiseman's planning template is a good starting point for your teen as they plan ahead.

Planning Template

Sit down with your teen and discuss planning their goals. Using a blank sheet of paper, ask them to consider the following points:

1. **What is your ultimate goal?**
   My ultimate goal is to ...
2. **Create a stage-by-stage plan.**
   Break your ultimate goal into five measurable stages. These stages should be realistic, specific and time-bound. As you look at these stages, think about how you will achieve them and how you will reward yourself. The rewards could be a trip to the hairdresser, buying an item of clothing, upgrading a mobile phone or renting a movie.
   Stage 1
   > My first sub-goal is to ...
   > I believe I can achieve this goal because ...
   > To achieve this sub-goal, I will ...
   > This will be achieved by the following date ...
   > My reward for achieving this will be ...

   Stage 2
   > My second sub-goal is to ...
   > I believe I can achieve this goal because ...
   > To achieve this sub-goal, I will ...
   > This will be achieved by the following date ...
   > My reward for achieving this will be ...

Stage 3

 My third sub-goal is to ...

 I believe I can achieve this goal because ...

 To achieve this sub-goal, I will ...

 This will be achieved by the following date ...

 My reward for achieving this will be ...

Stage 4

 My fourth sub-goal is to ...

 I believe I can achieve this goal because ...

 To achieve this sub-goal, I will ...

 This will be achieved by the following date ...

 My reward for achieving this will be ...

Stage 5

 My fifth sub-goal is to ...

 I believe I can achieve this goal because ...

 To achieve this sub-goal, I will ...

 This will be achieved by the following date ...

 My reward for achieving this will be ...

3. **What are the benefits of achieving your ultimate goal?**

   List three benefits of achieving your goal. How will life be better for you, your family and society when you achieve your overall goal?

   Benefit 1: _____

   Benefit 2: _____

   Benefit 3: _____

4. **Going public.**

   Who are you going to tell about your goal? Could you post it on your Facebook page or blog about it? Could you put it somewhere visible in the house, above your desk, on the fridge, on the mirror?

   I will go public by: _____

Hollie's Planning Template
This is how Transition Year student Hollie set out her template.

1. **What is your ultimate goal?**

   My overall goal is to develop and improve myself in Transition Year.

2. **Create a stage-by-stage plan.**

   Stage 1

   My first sub-goal is to *get to know the world of work better.*

   I believe I can achieve this goal because *I will give things a go and I am determined to come out of my comfort zone.*

   To achieve this sub-goal, I will *research and ask for work experience in the busiest veterinary practice.*

   This will be achieved by *early October.*

   My reward for achieving this will be *gaining insight and knowledge into veterinary medicine as a career.*

   Stage 2

   My second sub-goal is to *improve my confidence.*

   I believe I can achieve this goal because *in Transition Year I will have to throw myself into classes and work together with new people.*

   To achieve this sub-goal, I will *open myself to new experiences such as drama performances.*

   This will be achieved by *September.*

   My reward for achieving this will be *partaking in drama competitions and having fun in rehearsals.*

   Stage 3

   My third sub-goal is to *get a Distinction in my piano exams and learn pieces outside the exams.*

   I believe I can achieve this goal because *I will have more time to practise in the evenings during Transition Year.*

To achieve this sub-goal, I will *practise for an hour every evening*.

This will be achieved by *December 2015*.

My reward for achieving this will be *enjoying new pieces such as 'Bohemian Rhapsody'*.

Stage 4

My fourth sub-goal is to *explore my career direction*.

I believe I can achieve this goal because *I want to be happy in my future work*.

To achieve this sub-goal, I will *work with vets, explore work experience in a zoo, explore a Plan B by looking at different career areas. I will try a variety of subjects with an open mind*.

This will be achieved by *April, when I pick my subjects*.

My reward for achieving this goal will be *more motivation and feeling focused in 5th Year*.

Stage 5

My fifth sub-goal is to *try new things and have more fun*.

I believe I can achieve this goal because *there are lots of opportunities in Transition Year*.

To achieve this sub-goal, I will *do drama, learn to surf, organise a traditional music concert, do a week's language exchange in France*.

This will be achieved by *May next year*.

My reward for achieving this will be *having fun, making friends, opening up a new world*.

3. **What are the benefits of achieving your ultimate goal?**

Benefit 1: *Feeling more prepared for 5th Year, able to focus better after having had a break from studies*.

Benefit 2: *Increased confidence – being more open and adaptable to people and situations*.

Benefit 3: *Knowing myself better, being aware of my likes and dislikes*.

4. **Going public.**

I will go public by *telling my friends and recording it in my Transition Year blog.*

Remember!

A Chinese philosopher once said, 'We achieve the great task by a series of small acts.'

Procrastination

Many teenagers I work with fall behind in achieving their goals by postponing timelines and study plans, procrastinating and therefore making inadequate preparations for the exams. Some teenagers in the Leaving Certificate year will say, 'I'll study after Hallowe'en', and then Hallowe'en becomes Christmas. Before they know it, the mock exams are upon them. Some say, 'I'll study after the mocks' or 'after Easter', and all of a sudden it's exam time and they haven't studied. Many delay focusing on their goals because they get sidetracked by distractions such as texting, Facebook, having an online presence, friends, the TV, or just hanging out with their friends. Some simply have a short attention span. Some students tell me that they text during class and this affects their ability to concentrate. Many tell me that they spend two to three hours a night on Facebook or playing computer games and this time eats into time available for study. It's worth noting that too much 'screen time' – whether on an iPhone, computer or TV – just before bed can interrupt sleep throughout the night. Obviously, phone messages and email notifications at night also disrupt sleep.

Procrastination can stem from feelings of low self-worth or a feeling of not being good enough. A fear of failure, a belief that talent and success are instantaneous, being unrealistic about goals and about what is required to achieve them can all hinder a teenager.

For some, there is also peer pressure, a need to act as if life is one big party where there is no room for serious action. A few years ago, I encountered a few students who felt it was better not to try at all, because failure through making no effort would not reflect their abilities. They thought that they would lose less face by not trying and then failing, rather than really trying and maybe failing.

Where procrastination is a problem, I suggest that the students study for a short period – perhaps only twenty minutes – to start off with. Research has shown that doing a task for just a few minutes is a good way of beating procrastination.

Typically, when students are making slower progress than desired with their ultimate goals I ask them: 'What do you need to **start doing** in order **to get the results you want**?' Some of the typical responses are:
- Start eating healthily
- Start eating breakfast
- Start joining in the homework club
- Start a study plan
- Start making mind maps and taking proper notes
- Start listening in class
- Start sitting beside a good studier at school
- Hand over the laptop to my Mum or Dad in the evening.

When I ask, 'What do you need to **stop doing** in order **to get the results you want**?', typical responses include:
- Stop using Facebook at night
- Stop worrying
- Stop drinking Coke
- Stop using my mobile phone in class and while doing my homework

- Stop hanging out with my mates so much
- Stop working so much at my part-time job
- Stop doing my homework in the kitchen.

My students get great clarity around the habits which can help or hinder their progress by answering these questions. These days, young people are influenced by *The X Factor,* Premier League football, reality TV programmes such as *Big Brother* and notions of instant success. When setting goals, it is really important not to have a 'Pollyanna' or rose-tinted approach to them, but also to look at what might get in the way of success. By writing down the things that might hinder their success you can help your teen identify possible setbacks. Then you could look at actions that could overcome and inoculate against setbacks.

My goal is: _____	
What could get in the way of achieving my goal?	*How can I avoid these setbacks?*
1. Going on Facebook	1. Give my laptop to Mum or Dad
2. Staying up late at night	2. Going to bed early
3.	3.
4.	4.

Inspiration

Motivation (derived from the Latin word *motivatus*, which means 'to move') is connected with **doing** something; inspiration (*inspiridus* or 'spirit') is connected with **being** something. Inspiration is the coating around motivation. Inspiration gives us a boost towards action.

Ann Marie was inspired by the work of Veronica Guerin, a journalist who was murdered for documenting gang crime in

Dublin. In reading about Veronica Guerin and her courageous spirit, Ann Marie decided to pursue a career in photojournalism so that she could uncover the truth and tell it through words and photo images.

Inspiration touches our hearts and spirits. If a young person is inspired to live out a certain purpose, this is the highest form of motivation. At the same time, the wells of inspiration need to be fed regularly, for example by nature, music, art, visits to college open days, history tours or trips to workplaces of interest. Of course the inspiration needs to be relevant to the young person's interests.

Eoin's Story

Five years ago, I brought a group of young people to visit the Dublin Fire Service Emergency and Training Centre. One final year student, Eoin Fogarty, said it was the most inspiring school trip he had ever been on, as from a young age he had wanted to be a firefighter. For this student, trying on the uniform, using the hydrant, and seeing the various types of equipment used in accidents set his heart on fire and confirmed for him his life dream. His inspiration made it easier for him to engage in community activities such as the Red Cross and first aid courses; to improve his fitness levels and achieve the points he needed to, in order to do a course prior to applying for the next round of recruitment. The stiff competition for places did not deter him and he was determined to be true to his inspired calling.

But while Eoin's heart was set on joining the Fire Service, he did have a Plan B. I followed up on his progress four years later. This is what he told me.

'I had my eye fixed on the Dublin Fire Service but they were not recruiting and rather than sit around waiting for them to recruit, I decided to gain more skills. Sport and coaching are big loves of mine and I played hurling and Gaelic for St Finbarr's. Fitness and optimum performance matters to me. I am delighted now with my choices. At 21, I now have a degree in Sports Management and Coaching. I'm considering doing an internship with the academy teams of football teams such as Arsenal or Sheffield United or even the Cambridge rugby team.

'Since I left school, I have remained motivated and proactive. Throughout college, I coached children with special needs and taught PE in a school. I continued to play hurling and Gaelic and work at my local club. As for studies, I took a steady, planned approach and did not leave everything until the last moment. My grades reflected my consistent efforts well.

'Outside college, it gave me great satisfaction to share my specialist knowledge and learning with my local teams. My knowledge of training, nutrition and psychology has benefited my team and made me a better player. The Fire Service is still on my radar and perhaps in the future they will recruit. In the meantime, I have no time to waste and I am happily focused on performance coaching!'

List the ways in which your teenager could feed his or her inspiration.

1. _____

2. _____

3. _____

Learning needs to be put into context and to be made fun. French in the classroom may seem irrelevant, but a period spent in France might inspire a teenager's love and aptitude for the language.

Likewise, a visit to the Gaeltacht will make the Irish language a living language and one associated with other young people and fun. A visit to a science exhibition might help your teen put a principle into context. Going to a theatre production or seeing screen versions of plays or novels on the English curriculum could make them seem more relevant.

Motivating teenagers is no easy task and it may take many different approaches to get them engaged; however, the best approach is to get them to seek motivation from their inner dream. See the 'Creativity' section of the Further Resources at the end of the book for some websites that give tips on how to do this.

Step 7 Key Points

- We are motivated either *towards* something or *away* from something.
- Inspiration is crucial for developing and achieving goals.
- You can better motivate your teenager if you are aware of the factors that influence your own motivation.
- Simple strategies can be used to help your teen to develop winning habits and increase their levels of motivation.
- Use the planning template with your teen to help them reach their goals.
- In order to beat procrastination, have your teenager identify what they can *start doing* in order to move closer to their goals.

❖

MY CAREER

Marie-Thérèse de Blacam
Co-Owner of Inis Meáin Restaurant & Suites,
Inis Meáin, the Aran Islands
www.inismeain.com

Inis Meáin Restaurant & Suites is an intimate restaurant and luxury inn offering a unique hospitality experience, inspired by its remote location and the natural beauty of the Aran Islands. It has received extensive critical acclaim in the international press.

'Be active and take up any opportunity of interest that comes your way.'

How did your career in hospitality begin?
Through a degree in Entrepreneurship, which gave me some of the skills and confidence needed to start my own business, which is something I always knew I wanted to do. Hospitality – because I married a chef!

Did you always want to do what you do now?
Own my own business? Yes. Do something creative? Yes. But beyond that, I had toyed over the years with thoughts of studying Architecture and I did study Fashion Design for four years by night while working in marketing after my Entrepreneurship degree. This allowed me to find my way into creative industries.

What do you enjoy most about what you do now?
The job satisfaction I get from giving people pleasure; and the control I have over my own life – to an extent – through working for myself.

What is the toughest thing about your job?
The long hours, financial insecurity (hopefully just in the initial years!), and the fact that you're always on call.

What motivates you?
I'm motivated to have a well-balanced life, to have sufficient time off work to enjoy raising our family, to enjoy work and to be sufficiently remunerated from it in order for our family to be financially secure and comfortable.

Who or what inspired you along the way?
My father, who set up his own business at 21 and has maintained it successfully for almost forty years.

What advice on getting started would you give young people who want a career in the same field?
For starting your own business, I would say try to take a year off to plan it as thoroughly as possible. For hospitality, location is of tremendous importance.

What has been the biggest lesson in your career to date?
Be prepared, front load work so that you have the capability to deal with the unexpected – which *will* happen!

If you had a motto, what would it be?
Live life to the full and make sure to enjoy the journey!

What advice would you give your 16-year-old self?
Be active and take up any opportunity of interest that comes your way. CV building through interesting activities and character development projects in teenage years can help open doors at the very start of your career. When researching careers, make sure to research not just the subject matter of the job, but also the lifestyle that it allows, i.e. pay scale, holidays, stress, travelling, etc. Try to weigh up the package that each career offers by putting these factors into the mix; hopefully you will find the bundle that best suits your preferences and personality.

❖

Five Ways to Try Out the World of Work

Before you go climbing the ladder of success you have got to make sure it is leaning up against the right wall.

ANONYMOUS

Trying out the world of work is a crucial part of your teen's career planning. It involves trying on careers for size and seeing if they fit. All career dreams should be tested for suitability. You wouldn't just buy a car from a showroom or off a catalogue; you'd take it for a test drive, get a feel for it and see if it fits your needs. Career choice also needs research and exploration. Through research, carrying out informational interviewing, networking and gaining work experience, your teen will learn more about which careers will suit them and which ones won't. Trying out the world of work will help them make informed choices and will save *you* the cost of them dropping out of college courses and changing direction.

Steps 1–7 should have armed your teen with good self-knowledge. Step 8 will help you guide your teen in exploring possibilities in the world of work through:

- Researching careers and jobs
- Speaking to people about their work
- Networking and practising an 'elevator speech'
- Work shadowing
- Gaining work experience

- Volunteering
- Working on areas of low confidence.

Dropping Out

The Economic and Social Research Institute (ESRI) reported in August 2014 that almost half of young people regretted their career choice. This finding was similar to an earlier Higher Education Authority (HEA) report (*A Study of Progression in Irish Higher Education*) that noted a 40 per cent dropout rate among students in some third-level courses. Reasons why students leave courses prematurely can include inadequate prior research into course choice; lack of consideration given to individual suitability for a course in terms of personal aptitude, interests and skills; and a lack of awareness of the planned career area and the work it involves.

Dropping out of third-level courses or apprenticeships can be very expensive. All courses involve some degree of cost, and for some (for example private beauty courses, physical therapy and hairdressing) you have to pay fees. Students who wish to drop out of a particular course and do not de-register before Christmas in their first year may be subject to full fees the following year. Also, students who receive a maintenance grant and have their registration fee paid for them and then drop out of first year do not qualify for the grant in the first year of a new course. For parents whose teenagers live away from home while at college, living costs can be anything from €7,000 to €10,000. All in all, changes in courses cost money.

Dropping out is also costly for the teenager in terms of their self-esteem as they can equate it with failure. In order to avoid this, it is really important that you help your child link into the world of work so that they have a realistic picture of what is involved in the career path they want to follow. As a result, they are more likely to start courses or jobs with their eyes wide open.

It's important to remember that **dropping out of a course does not define your teenager.** It is possible to regroup and make different and better choices in the future. According to the American Department of Labor, the average person has seven careers over their lifetime!

Here are five ways in which your teenager can explore the world of work. (More can be found in the 'Occupational Information' section in the list of Further Resources at the end of this book.)

1. Research and informational interviewing
2. Networking and introducing yourself
3. Work shadowing
4. Work experience
5. Volunteering and participation.

1. Research and Informational Interviewing

What's Out There Now?

In order to gain an informed view of the current world of work, your teen could do some investigative work by looking at the jobs market and at companies that are recruiting. You could both look online at job sites such as www.irishjobs.ie and www.monster.ie, or go through job advertisements in the paper. Here is a simple pen and paper task that you don't need any technology for:

TASK F: TACKLE THE JOBS PAGE!

Cut out jobs that may interest your teen and separate them into (a) roles that look interesting and (b) employers that look interesting.

Write down attributes associated with each job. Create cards based on these individual attributes. Group them under each job position. For example, let's say you find ads for an ambulance driver, firefighter, driver and tour guide, all of which your teen is interested in. Start with the ambulance driver and separate out the individual parts of what it is about the role of ambulance driver that grabs your teen's interest, e.g. saving lives, working under pressure, driving, working with a team of paramedics, working in a fast-paced environment, etc.

Now go back to the other ads and find the common themes in the jobs. In the above example they might be helping others, being on the move, variety, working under pressure and so on. Have a conversation about each job and discuss the patterns you see that are common to all jobs.

The Internet

It is all very well for your teen to want to pursue a career as a journalist, soldier, pilot, etc., but do they really know what is involved in the day-to-day job? One of the quickest and easiest ways to get an insight into how a job area or industry works is to visit the websites of professional associations, trade unions or educational/training organisation relevant to the career fields that interest your teen most.

These sites can list industry information, required qualifications, jobs, useful contacts and upcoming events related to the industry that your teen might be able to attend.

Informational Interviewing

Ideally, the best ways to gain a realistic insight into what is involved in any particular job or field is to speak to someone who works in that occupational area. So how do you go about identifying them and contacting them?

First explore your own personal contacts and those of your teenager: family, friends, work colleagues, people in your community, etc. Make a list of the people who might be able to shed some light on the career ideas that your teenager has and ask them if they would be willing to speak to/be interviewed by your teen about their jobs.

Second, if your teen has identified an area of interest that you have no contacts in, use the internet to investigate whether that career area has a professional organisation that your teenager could contact with a view to asking the organisation if they could put them in contact with someone who would be willing to speak to/ be interviewed by your child about their job. For example, if your child is interested in the property market, they could contact either of the two associations for professional auctioneers and valuers. Most professional organisations are only to willing to help.

With your teen, list the people they could ask about their careers:

1. _____

2. _____

3. _____

What Questions to Ask?

There are tips later in the chapter on how your teen can make an initial introduction, but what exactly does your teen ask these people once they agree to speak to/be interviewed by them? Your teen's aim should be to find out as much information about the job that is relevant to them.

Here is a list of questions your teen could use for an informational interview:

- What is good or interesting about your job?
- How did you come to be working in your job?
- What is a typical day?
- What is difficult about your job?

- Have you any recommendations for people wanting to get into this area?
- What are the responsibilities of your job?
- What skills, qualities and abilities are helpful in this occupation?
- What particular training or employment experience is needed for this work?
- If you were to go back in time, would you choose this occupation again?
- What are the opportunities for advancement in this occupation?
- What is the typical starting salary for someone in this line of work?
- Can you give me any advice on where to access more information about this work, or could you recommend anyone who could help me do more research?

If your teen knows the contact well enough, and if it is appropriate to ask for a favour, they could ask the following questions, but consider them wisely:

- Are there any opportunities for work shadowing or volunteering with you?
- Who else would be good to talk to?
- Would it be possible to let me know if any part-time work comes up in your area?

Encourage your teen to show a genuine interest in the contact and in what they have to say. Let them know that their advice is valued and make sure that your teen follows up with a thank you email or card.

2. Networking and Introducing Yourself

Networking is all about relationship building. According to the Oxford English Dictionary, 'networking' is 'Interacting with others to exchange information and develop professional or social contacts.' Networking is central to the changing world of work. As a parent you need to foster the networking habit in your teen. It is an effective way to research career areas, source work experience and help your teen gain advice about entry and application processes. Networking can happen anytime and anywhere. Friends, family, colleagues and the internet are good places to start.

The concept of networking is daunting for many, but it is really just about having conversations with people and seeing whether either person can help the other. If your teen has a prepared introduction about themselves that they can say with ease, it will help them feel more comfortable about networking and about asking for work, work experience, Transition Year placements and other opportunities. Some teens are naturally more outgoing than others, but whether your teen is an introvert or an extrovert, crafting and practising a short introduction or 'elevator pitch' about themselves can help immensely in overcoming nerves.

Introductions or 'Elevator Pitches'

The popular term 'elevator pitch' comes from the studio days of Hollywood, when a screenwriter would share a lift with an unsuspecting executive. There, within the confines of the elevator, the screenwriter would 'pitch' an idea for a film to the decision-maker in one minute, before the lift reached their floor. These days, the term has become popular among professionals to describe how they introduce themselves and their products or services.

I have encountered teenagers who were too shy to pick up the phone to ask for job leads or information about a career area.

I once had a client called Christopher who wanted to be a hairdresser. At 17, Christopher was too shy to speak to a

127

hairdresser on the phone or to follow up on leads. At the time I was really concerned about his shyness, as I felt it was holding him back. Thankfully, five years later I hear that he is running a hairdressing salon. His confidence has soared since the age of 17.

It is possible to overcome shyness, but it takes practice. Even if your teen isn't particularly shy, practising the following steps will help build their capacity to network and make connections in the future. Here's a guide to help your teen get started on their own 'elevator pitch':

> Hello, my name is (*first and last name*) _____.
> I am a student at _____, where I am in (*course of study or year in school*) _____. I am really interested in _____ (*specific area*).
> I am also involved in (*extra-curricular activities or interests*)
> _____. Since you are a professional in (*name of field*) _____, I would really love the chance to talk to you about your own experience in this field. Would you be willing to speak with me some time for twenty minutes about the work you do?

If you get a positive response, follow it up with: 'When would be the best time to call or email you?' and then, 'Thank you. I will contact you on _____ (*time/day you will follow up*).'

Shake their hand and write a follow-up email as soon as you can.

If the person responds negatively, back off from your request and simply say, 'Well, thanks for taking the time to listen. Take care.'

If your teen does get a negative response, remind them not to take it too personally.

This approach can be adapted to use on the phone or in an email if you decide to make your initial contact through one of those modes of communication instead. This type of approach can also be used if your teen is looking for work experience or job shadowing. See Appendix 1 for a more detailed and structured version of how to network.

3. Work Shadowing

Find out if it is possible for your child to **work shadow** a professional for a day. Shadowing involves closely observing someone at work doing a particular role, rather than taking on the role yourself. This process gives a good insight into the reality of the job. Time and again, young people choose careers that require high points, such as dentistry, pharmacy and speech therapy, without really having a clear sense of what is involved in the work. Shadowing offers the opportunity to ask plenty of questions similar to the ones outlined in the section about informational interviewing. Make a list of people your teen could ask to shadow.

Whether your teen is simply shadowing a professional for the day or is volunteering their time on an ongoing basis, it is important to record their impressions of what they observe. Sometimes there are factors in an occupational setting that will matter to them that they didn't find in their online research or informational interviews.

One first-year pharmacy student I met did not like her course. During our conversation, it emerged that she had never looked for work experience or work shadowed a pharmacist. Her entire focus had been on getting high points in the Leaving Cert and she had never seen the relevance of testing out the world of pharmacy. It was only when she decided to leave her course that she began to explore thoroughly what careers and courses really interested her.

---

4. Work Experience

Work experience gives your teenager a chance to 'try before they buy' into investing years of their life in a particular career path. For example, working on a help desk or in the catering section of an airport might give someone a feel for what it might be like to be ground staff or an air steward. The benefits of securing work experience while in Transition Year or during the summer months include:

- Gaining insight into different industries, work practices and work environments
- Having the chance to develop employable skills such as customer awareness, people skills, problem-solving, teamwork, communication skills and leadership
- Opportunities for employment in the future with the work experience employer
- Opportunities to make contacts and meet professionals in the field
- Learning more about a job, which can confirm a career plan or prompt a reassessment.

Encourage and help your teen get a part-time entry-level job, ideally in a field that interests them. They will then experience the workplace setting first hand and gain experience that they can list on their CV. They can use networking skills to find part-time employment by approaching employers directly. For example, a part-time job in the RTÉ/BBC canteen will give them an insight into careers in television, radio and the media.

A 2010 survey by jobs website gradireland.com asked employers what they felt were effective ways to improve graduates' transferable skills (i.e. skills that can be moved from one area to another):

> Overwhelmingly, 94 per cent replied that a work placement represented an effective method followed closely by team-based activities at college and taking leadership positions in clubs and societies. (John Walshe, 'Employers say graduates can't write well enough', *Irish Independent,* 11 October 2010)

This survey underlines the value of gaining work experience, not only to try out the world of work but also to build employability.

I would recommend that, ideally, your teen chooses a workplace of excellence and works alongside an expert. In that way they can 'model' or copy the behaviour of those who are the best at their jobs.

A Word on Mentoring

'Mentoring' refers to a relationship where a more experienced person helps a less knowledgeable person. A mentor might be found among your circle of immediate friends and family, at school, in your community or within your field of interest. In Generation 21 research conducted by Dublin City University, being mentored was seen as the second most effective way after work experience of fostering attributes sought by employers among graduates (www. dcu.ie/generation21/index.shtml). The other attributes identified in the report included being creative/enterprising, solution oriented, an effective communicator, globally engaged, active leaders and committed to continuous learning.

Michelle Obama, the First Lady of the United States, when she was a young girl growing up in a low-income area of Chicago, was mentored by a passionate, professional woman who cared about community service. Today, Michelle Obama has paired twenty young women with twenty female mentors in the President's Office. She wants teenage girls to be inspired, confident in their abilities and able to speak to people in power without fear.

So as a parent it would be wise to introduce this concept even at secondary level. Mentors can help teens with decision-making processes, understand their strengths and help them build on them. Most important, mentoring can help teens develop social skills.

5. Volunteering and Participation

Volunteering enables young people to build concrete experience in a variety of areas – youth work, social work, administration, event management, marketing, research. Young people can use volunteering as a means to investigating potential career paths and/or to understanding our society better. It also allows an opportunity to clarify one's own passions and interests, build and realise strengths and to address any skills gaps. (Roísín McGrogan, former Civic Engagement Officer, Trinity College, Dublin)

Volunteer Ireland saw a 100 per cent increase in inquiries in 2010. Even if your child does not secure paid part-time work, volunteering is a great way for them to build their confidence, maturity and self-reliance. It demonstrates to future employers that your teenager has communication skills and interpersonal skills and can work in a team.

It provides an opportunity to get a real insight into a particular career area, raising their self-awareness regarding their suitability to the area, and gives them the opportunity to build contacts for the future. It also develops such qualities as empathy and having compassion for others.

Involvement in extra-curricular activities at school or in

Transition Year projects is another great way for teenagers to develop personal passions while simultaneously gaining life and employment skills along the way. Participation in An Gaisce or the Prince's Trust can help your teen to: increase their confidence; develop planning abilities, organisational and teamwork skills; help with goal setting; and foster a sense of achievement.

Here are some suggestions of activities your teen could volunteer for or participate in:

- Transition Year projects, e.g. Start Your Own Business projects
- An Gaisce (the President's Award) and the Prince's Trust programmes
- Local youth clubs
- Summer camps for younger children
- School plays and concerts
- School or class committees.

List some other places where your teen could volunteer:

- _____
- _____
- _____

Eannain's Story

As a university student Eannain Strain volunteered with the Samaritans. Here he explains why he did it and how he benefited from the experience of helping others.

'I began to think about joining the Samaritans on the advice of the career development centre in Magee (Co. Derry) when I was there at university.

'I was looking for experience of a counselling type, and was having trouble getting any observational experience through the HSE or with any qualified psychologists.

'In the first semester of second year I called to the local Samaritans centre. As with any applicant they called me for interview, which included asking me what my reasons were for joining the Samaritans. I told them that I would have about three years to contribute to the service and in return I would like the experience and perhaps a reference! They seemed happy enough with that. I attended training, which was thorough, and began the probationary period immediately after that. Training lasted about six weeks and consisted of reading, watching DVDs, listening to audio examples and role playing. Probation consisted of observing current volunteers, exposure to callers, and asking questions "on the job".

'For approximately the next four years, I volunteered for three and a half hours once a week, with an overnight session every month. Towards the end I became a trainer for the current volunteers. Every current volunteer was required to undergo at least three hours of ongoing training each year. For this role, I had to design and deliver different training sessions to address specific issues that the centre was experiencing at a local and national level – e.g. how to deal with a certain type of caller known locally, or how to deal with high call volumes.'

The benefits

'This type of volunteering experience gave me excellent exposure to a very wide section of society. Literally any member of the community could call the Samaritans, so I was in contact with all sorts of demographics. I believe that this was a huge benefit over other types of experience because of the chance to speak to all sections of society. From a purely selfish point of view, I used this experience to see which groups I wanted to work with, e.g. old people, teenagers, divorcees, any minority groups, etc. – the list is endless.

'Again, from a selfish point of view, because of the huge variety of issues callers brought to the centre, I got to see which kind of issues I would most like to work with. I could see fairly quickly which issues/demographics I wanted to help in my own career (and what I didn't want!). This definitely helped me choose a career area to focus on for the future.

'The experience was excellent. The regular volunteer experience taught me to develop communication skills; how to control expression of my own opinion; how to leave the job (and everything about it) behind me when I went home in the evening; patience; how to interpret what people mean without the benefit of seeing their body language (i.e. via the phone); assertiveness, the ability to create a connection with people from all backgrounds regardless of their state of mind and how to support team members. With the extra responsibility of designing training sessions for the current volunteers I had to develop leadership skills (e.g. leading the training session), organising the classes, chairing discussions, selling ideas to the group, etc.'

Eannain is now a careers adviser working in Student Services at Maynooth University.

See Further Resources, 'Year Out/Volunteering', at the end of this book for contacts and sources of information on volunteering.

TASK G: WORKING ON AREAS OF LOW CONFIDENCE

Encourage your child to self-assess when looking at jobs of interest and to identify areas where they don't feel confident about their knowledge or experience. Then get them to build strategies to gain that confidence. If, for example, they are looking at sports management, and teamwork skills are highlighted, but they don't feel comfortable in teams, get them to think of ways in which they can participate in teams or group projects in their local area. Something like a part-time job in the local pizzeria or café, for example, can build confidence in dealing with people they don't know and teach them how to work in a team to deliver a result.

If they have an interest in entrepreneurship and enterprise they will need an understanding of entrepreneurial skills. You might encourage them to get involved in the Transition Year Start Your Own Business project; take them to a small enterprise convention; get them to think of ways of making money in their locality; or enter a Young Enterprise competition, such as the Mini Company, which can help unlock a teenager's business awareness. The Network for Teaching Entrepreneurship, NFTE (pronounced Nifty), can help young people develop their entrepreneurial creativity.

Here's the story of a 15-year-old girl who is now the owner of a thriving business – Rosso Solini's Designer Soles.

The 15-Year-Old Entrepreneur

Like many teenage girls, Tara Haughton was an avid reader of fashion magazines and aware of the famous red soles that are the signature of shoe designer Christian Louboutin. In 2010, while at a family wedding, red confetti stuck to the soles of Tara's shoes, which were still sticky after she had removed the price tag. Later, at the wedding reception, a woman asked Tara if she was wearing Louboutin shoes.

And so a great business idea was born. For a school project, Tara researched the possibility of manufacturing 'fake' red soles that could be stuck to the bottom of women's shoes to give the Louboutin look without the $2000 price tag. Eventually, she sourced funding and a manufacturer and now owns her own shop, which exports worldwide, creates jobs and has won multiple awards. See www.rossosolinishop.com/.

Research, informational interviewing, work shadowing, work experience and volunteering will all help your child to learn and experience the pros and cons of a typical day in a particular job, either directly or as an observer. They can then process what parts of the job they like and dislike and see if they can imagine themselves in that position. They can reflect on whether it is in line with their dream for themselves. Last, but not least, they can decide if they are prepared to take the action required to get into that position.

Step 8 Key Points
- Through networking, work shadowing, work experience and volunteering, your teen will improve their interpersonal, communication and problem-solving skills and their networking ability and flexibility.
- Inappropriate course and career choices can cost money and negatively affect your teen's confidence.
- Researching career areas and jobs can mitigate against this.
- Research is best if it is practical and experiential, e.g. informational interviewing, work shadowing, work experience.
- It is important that your teen learns to be comfortable networking. Crafting and practising an introduction or 'elevator speech' about themselves will help them with nerves and speaking to people they don't know.
- Volunteering helps build confidence and skills that will make your teen more employable in the future.

Congratulations! You now have a range of methods to help your teen fully test out the world of work.

❖

MY CAREER

Peter McAlindon
Director, McAlindon Wine
www.directwineshipments.com

Direct Wine Shipments (DWS) is Belfast's oldest independent wine merchant, having traded since 1954. The McAlindon family has produced their own wine, Creu Celta. DWS was awarded Best Independent Wine Retailer in 2013.

> *'Don't be precious. Do whatever it takes to build your CV – from filling shelves to mopping the floor – if required. Be keen and show initiative. It will eventually be noticed.'*

How did your career in wine importing begin?

By accident, really. I had worked in the family off licence business when I was young, on Saturdays and during the holidays. I never thought I would end up in the family business. I didn't really work that hard for my O and A Levels, though I still managed to scrape into university. I was really unfocused and rebellious at this time. I wanted to take a year out after leaving school but my parents disapproved. It wasn't the common thing at the time, but a year off would probably have given me a bit of space to work out what I really wanted to do. I was going to get a job stacking shelves to save money and then I would have travelled.

Anyway, I made a mess of university, dropped out and went back to working in the family off licence. After a while, I got interested in wine and started doing Wine and Spirit Education

Trust (WSET) exams. WSET was set up in the 1950s to educate people going into the wine trade. I passed one exam and then signed up and passed the two-year diploma. This is of degree standard. Passing these exams gave me knowledge, confidence and effectively made me a wine merchant.

Did you always want to do what you do now?

No I didn't. I think I gradually grew into it and the more I learned, the more it took a grip on me and as time passed, the better I became at the job. Wine is a very interesting subject. It encompasses, history, geography, science, travel, culture, food and it's very pleasurable (in moderation of course!).

What do you enjoy most about what you do now?

I run the business with my brother. We both made a pact years ago to support each other and this has made our achievements happen quicker. The fact that I am my own boss is important. I would find it very difficult to work for someone else, particularly at this stage in my life.

My job is varied and that makes it stimulating (and frustrating!). I'm not doing the same thing day in and day out. I also work with a good team of people who work hard, have bought in to what we are trying to do and most of them have a sense of humour.

What is the toughest thing about your job?

There have been various issues over the years. Personnel difficulties are often stressful, but thankfully we have very few of these problems these days. A few years ago, we had some financial difficulties, dropping sales and sliding profits. A road closure (for three years) turned our building from being beside a very busy road to being in a cul-de-sac. This was very challenging and required a united response from the whole team. We had to make one person redundant, have a salary freeze for over three years, get rid of some staff benefits and really reduce costs. We started a new wholesale business and we all rolled our sleeves up. Thankfully, this strategy worked and we have been growing year on year for the past five years.

What motivates you?
We are a small specialist company, so winning tenders against larger organisations always gives me a thrill. We are fiercely independent and have had no help from government subsidies, etc. Finding new wines from up and coming regions or wine producers. Giving good presentations to customers.

Who or what inspired you along the way?
Various people. My father, his business consultant (a wise old Scottish accountant who was very clear and direct) and people in sport who have really achieved, especially against the odds and for long periods of time. We often talk about a company being like a football team. All of us are vital to being successful. All of us need to work, contribute and help each other, then we will all benefit.

We were voted the Best Independent Wine Retailer in the UK in November 2013. This was a first for a Northern Irish company. This was a team effort from everyone involved today and in the past.

What advice on getting started would you give young people who want a career in the same field?
If you really want to go into the wine business, work in retail first. Study for WSET qualifications, either by yourself or maybe with a company that encourages you. Travel and visit wine-

growing regions. Try to get a job working in a winery. During 'vintage time' is best, as they need a big influx of people to help at this busy time. This is when you may actually have an opportunity to get a job for a few weeks. Don't be precious. Do whatever it takes to build your CV – from filling shelves to mopping the floor if required. Be keen and show initiative. It will eventually be noticed. When you are younger, it's good to serve an apprenticeship, to learn the ropes from older, more experienced people. Watch and listen.

What has been the biggest lesson in your career to date?
Not giving in.

If you had a motto, what would it be?
Never give up, do the best you can and try to have a laugh along the way.

What advice would you give your 16-year-old self?
Maximise your potential. Work really hard and get the best grades you can. It will put you in good stead going forward. It will also give you good habits. Your education and working life is like a game of snakes and ladders. Avoid the snakes and go up the ladders. Work hard and you will really enjoy your free time.

Try to have varied interests, i.e. sporting, cultural, etc. I didn't work hard enough in my youth and this meant it took a lot longer for me to do well in a career, but I did get there in the end. So if you are finding the pressures of work, essay/project deadlines mounting up and it's all getting to you, don't give up, you'll get there in the end.

❖

Helping Your Teen Build Inner Strength and Resilience

Obstacles, of course, are developmentally necessary; they teach kids strategy, patience, critical thinking, resilience and resourcefulness.

NAOMI WOLF

I t's all very well to discover with your teen the 'work they were born to do', but no matter how much career planning is done, you need to prepare them for the fact that things do not always go according to plan. Your child will be competing in a global market. The teenagers in countries such as China and India are accustomed to strict discipline, stiff competition and rigorous demands. These teenagers are highly resilient and well able to bounce back from setbacks.

Life can throw us a curve ball at any point in our lives. The important thing is that we respond to these changes and events in ways that turn them to our advantage. Therefore, equipping your child to cope with change and overcome setbacks is crucial to career success, happiness and overall wellbeing. Having conversations about the importance of good coping skills and persistence will increase your teen's resilience and inner strength; it will give them more confidence to take courageous action in their lives and careers. In her *Irish Times* article '"We'll fix it": Parents do their children no favours', Sheila Wayman quotes Dr Tony Bates, psychologist and founding director of Headstrong, the National Centre for Youth Mental Health: 'parents would love to spare their children all pain and suffering, but that is not going to happen.' He says that the best thing we can is to equip children to deal with adversity. For Tony Bates, resilience in a young person means that by age 17 or 18, they have a good sense of self – who they are, what works for them and what doesn't, and awareness of their strengths and vulnerable areas. The same article treats of the dangers of over-parenting, over-intervening, being overly generous and rushing in to fix things for children. This style of parenting fails to recognise that children have to cope with unhappiness in order to be happy.

Step 9:

- Introduces the notion that change is constant, both in work and in life
- Shows the importance of familiarising your teen with change and learning to see change as an opportunity for growth
- Looks at how you can encourage your teen's strength and flexibility
- Offers examples of resilient young people
- Examines people who overcame adversity
- Encourages you to reflect on chance happenings and how change shaped your own career.

Helping your teen become comfortable with the idea of constant change will strengthen their ability to navigate successfully through the changing world of work. As an adolescent, your teen is developing and changing and they need to be confident in their own change. The more your teen can cope with change, meeting new people, joining new groups, going to new places, encountering different cultures, etc., the better they will manage sudden change. Where you can, praise your teen's ability to cope with change, handle new situations, overcome a setback, solve a problem or deal with an unexpected happening.

Some of the following strategies can help you enhance resilience in your child:

1. Jolanta Burke, positive psychologist at Trinity College, Dublin, advocates offering specific, positive feedback that praises the process – the effort and strategy – not the person. She says, 'If you praise a child for being smart, when they don't do well they automatically think it is because they are not smart' (*Irish Times*, 16 February 2015). Look back at the task 'Find the Gold and Polish it' in Step 1 on communication (page 29) to see examples of specific positive feedback.

2. Identify your child's coping mechanisms and refer to their ability to cope in the future. For example, 'You really handled that confrontation with your friend well. I liked the way you dealt with it honestly and fairly. I can see you will have the ability to handle any disputes or fallouts when they happen in the future.'

3. Encourage responsibility and self-efficacy. In other words, when things go wrong for your teen, get them to reflect and think aloud about what they could have done differently. Encourage them to have a sense of control of their situation and to focus on what they can control. For example, one teenager might see a poor result in a test or project as a reflection of their lack of intelligence. Another more optimistic child might view it as a lack of preparation and hard work. Learning from experience is the best education we get in life. Being able to reflect promotes a sense of wellbeing.

4. Encourage connections with others. Social support from friends, the wider family network, teachers and school guidance counsellors builds resilience. It is important to encourage your teen to express themselves and not to bottle things up inside.

5. Where appropriate, keeping a diary or a journal of positive

things about themselves or how they handled situations and coped can build a greater sense of self. Recently, I encouraged a 14-year-old girl who was battling with an eating disorder to do this as well as seeking professional help. Other teens may prefer to use art or music as a medium of expression.

6. Of course, if, as a parent, you feel that your teen is overwhelmed and is not coping, make sure they know it is okay for them to ask for help. There are many organisations, such as Headstrong, Jigsaw and other support agencies, who offer mental health supports to young people.

7. Volunteering, helping out at home or in the community can really promote a sense of belonging. Highlight their contribution or the role they play within the family or community.

8. Family rituals (mealtimes, walks, or a curry on a Friday night) can create a sense of comfort and security. Creating downtime with your teen allows them to spend time with you or themselves without structured activities.

Some years ago, I worked as a school guidance counsellor with a 16-year-old boy who had a poor sense of self. He did not feel confident and doubted himself due to his school grades and sports performance and he compared himself negatively to the other boys in his class who were more muscular and bigger in stature. I empathised with his feelings and pointed out that there were more qualities and talents within him. Together, we looked at activities that would give him meaning and confidence. I suggested that he might join the Civil Defence in Dublin, as this young man dreamed of a life in a Garda uniform. Some years later I received an email from him telling me about how confident he had become. This email touched my heart and brought tears to my eyes. He thanked me for pointing him towards the Civil Defence as it had really boosted his self-esteem. He described in detail the feeling of elation and pride he had had when he stood in uniform at Dublin Castle when the Dublin GAA team won the All Ireland. The young man in the email had become an entirely different man.

This example echoes the advice given by Betty McLaughlin, guidance counsellor at Colaiste Mhuire CBS, Mullingar. McLaughlin, President of the Institute of Guidance Counsellors, recommends that second-level students get involved in sports or some other activity in the community, thereby 'building up a little group for themselves so that when things go bad, they have someone to turn to' (quoted in Sheila Wayman's article in the *Irish Times*, 16 February 2015).

In her book *Flourishing*, psychologist Maureen Gaffney suggests the following:

Think back over your own life or, better still, draw a 'lifeline' across a page, with your birth at one end and your death at the other end. Now, mark out the different stages in your life, each with their high points, low points and transition points. By doing this, you may gain insights into your own resilience.

Gaffney points out that we have all lived through great economic and social uncertainty, unsure of the future. Yet we soldier on.

Reflect

Reflect on your own resilience and ability to cope with uncertainty.

TASK H: LIFELINE REVIEW

With your teen, get them to review their own lifeline, the ups and downs and, more important, the major transitions and decision points. Have them reflect on their ability to manage change, such as starting secondary school, moving school, taking up a sport, getting a part-time job, choosing subjects, taking up a project and so on. Help them value their own ability to cope with the unknown and their confidence that they will adapt to the workplace or to college later on.

This year I worked with a 17-year-old girl who lost her father suddenly. This devastating event made her take her own life more seriously. She began to reflect on what her life was all about and decided to look into becoming a chef. She enrolled in cooking classes twice a week, which intensified her interest in cooking and helped her through her grief. She wanted to make her father proud of her and started attending open days and information events about the culinary arts. Before her father's death, this young woman had drifted and lacked interest in school and life. Now she was committed to making a good future for herself and her widowed mother.

Here are two of the features that psychologists have identified in resilient people:

1. **They identify and use role models**. They find a role model who encourages them and gives them comfort. In other words, having access to adults who believe in you and support you helps build resilience. As a parent you can draw on the support of relations, godparents, etc. to inspire, motivate and encourage your teenager. Perhaps your teenager might be more receptive to someone outside the family, even if the message is the same.

A teenager I know looked to her uncle as a role model. Her uncle was a photographer and he was able to show her the ropes of photography and give her encouragement. Another teenage boy I knew was into Gaelic football and hurling. He looked to his coach as a source of guidance in matters of the heart, friendship and life choices. He felt that he could confide in him better than anyone else. In many ways, his coach was central to his emotional development.

2. **They see frustrations and even trauma as challenges and opportunities to grow**, rather than be overtaken by self-pity or feelings of being overwhelmed. In other words, when setbacks or disappointments happen, resilient people see them as a chance to grow or learn something. For example, if a student doesn't get the points they need for a course, they can choose another route: do a PLC (Post Leaving Cert) course, an access course, or start with a Certificate or Diploma course and eventually achieve their goals (see Appendix 6 for more information on PLCs). Some may learn a practical skill and return to college as a mature student in their twenties.

The fashion designer Sir Paul Smith left school at 15 intent on being a professional racing cyclist. However, at 17 he had a serious accident that left him in hospital for months. During this time, he was introduced to art, design and photography. He began to see a new way ahead for himself. He enrolled in night classes in tailoring and opened a small shop. By the time he was 24, his collection was on the Paris catwalks. Today he is known worldwide and has showrooms in Tokyo, Milan and Paris.

A young man who lost his mother to cancer was inspired by her palliative care team and in particular by the contribution of the physiotherapist. His observations of the physiotherapist's work awoke in him a desire to pursue this path. In addition, as an attempt to cope with the loss of his mother he poured all his energy into rowing. He found rowing to be meditative and his mind was at peace when rowing. Within a few months of his mother's passing, he made it on to the national rowing team.

When we are bombarded with talk of recession on TV, radio, in newspapers and in conversation, awareness of our resilience is even more important. Negativity and fear can be overcome with open, positive communication, and a home environment where your child can talk about anything helps build their resilience. Resilience is an inner strength that helps develop flexibility. It is like a tree that is deeply rooted, withstanding any change in weather, high winds and storms. Flexibility is a vital part of the jigsaw for careers in the future, when contract work will become more common. You can build your child's resilience by parenting in a way that supports them in standing alone and apart from the crowd at times; that teaches them to trust their instincts/gut reactions and make good decisions based on them; and to reach out to others and benefit from their expertise.

Examples of Resilience

It is beneficial to focus on the resilience and resourcefulness of previous generations and tell stories that demonstrate the values and qualities of grandparents or past members of the community. Many of us can remember stories of how our grandparents got through the Depression years in the 1930s or how our parents managed unemployment in the 1960s and high taxation in the 1970s.

I found a great example of this in my locality in the foundation of the co-operative, 'The Cope', in Templecrone in County Donegal. In 1906, Paddy 'the Cope' Gallagher had a vision of bringing business and employment to the local area of Dungloe. The area had seen mass emigration to Scotland. Paddy's vision entailed harnessing electricity, manufacturing local craftwork and setting up shops and a builders' yard. Today, 'The Cope' employs a hundred people. My own grandfather committed his life to this movement that helped sustain the local community.

Biographies and autobiographies of people who remained positive in the face of adversity might encourage your child to emulate or copy some of their techniques.

TASK 1: PEOPLE WHO OVERCAME ADVERSITY

Bring biographies and autobiographies of people who remained positive in the face of adversity to the attention of your teen. This may encourage them to emulate some of the techniques used by others. For example, if your child watches *Top Gear*, presenter Richard Hammond's account of how he rehabilitated himself after a horrific accident could be of interest. Stories about President Obama, Nelson Mandela, Michael J. Fox, Terry Waite, Oprah Winfrey, J. K. Rowling, to name a few, could inspire your child to develop resilience. Suggest that they make the links between the lives of those role models and their own lives.

Jade O'Toole: An Example of Resilience

'When I did my Leaving Cert, I was hell-bent on becoming a guard. Most of all, I wanted to serve people. I had been in an accident and I was inspired and moved greatly by the courageous actions of a female guard. I was expecting to do well in college and I hoped to get a degree while waiting on Garda recruitment.

'Although I had been very optimistic, I didn't do great in the Leaving Cert and I was very disappointed. Having looked at my options, I decided to do a Post Leaving Cert course in Criminology and Social Studies. I felt that might be a good gateway into the Guards. However, while studying, I realised that this career would not suit my disposition, so I was back to square one yet again! I had to start over and think about ways to serve people in a manner that was in keeping with my values. Community development began to catch my attention and I felt that I could serve people in the community in a way that felt right to me.

'I progressed on to a degree in Social and Community Development. During my degree, I volunteered in St Vincent de Paul's Ozanam House and I led groups of fifteen children. I became a co-ordinator for their grinds school and I was able to apply my knowledge from this experience to my college course. In addition, I did a three-month placement in the Sanctuary with Sister Stan. I found the Sanctuary a very peaceful and respectful environment. I helped organise their databases and plan for a fundraiser concert in Croke Park. It was called "Stars, Choir and Carols" and 11,000 people attended, breaking a Guinness world record!

'In college, I found my groove and while my Leaving Cert results were very poor, I had the highest grades in my college course. This really boosted my confidence, which had been knocked after the Leaving Cert. My lecturers have already offered me the opportunity to study for a funded master's that is based on a research project.

Eventually, I'd like to do a doctorate. By helping others, I feel that I am helping myself.

'I would say to teenagers that on the one hand, my plans did not work out. I did not get the grades I expected. Doing a PLC ruled out the Guards for me and ruled in community development. However, studying what I am most interested in gave me the motivation and desire to do very well in the end. Most important, I have held on to my values of being of service and making a difference.'

Embrace the Unexpected

> Nothing is more dangerous than a dogmatic worldview – nothing more constraining, more blinding to innovation, more destructive of openness to novelty. (Stephen Jay Gould)

Encourage your child to be flexible and to keep their eyes open. Flexibility is an attribute that employers value. If your child is willing to be flexible, they will be prepared for the unexpected, capable of making changes when needed and able to embrace opportunities when they arise. Many chance encounters and meetings offer career changes, opportunities and leads. While we have discussed many ways of career planning, many of us are in jobs because we met someone who inspired us, gave us a chance or because we were in the right place at the right time.

An unemployed graduate who came to me for guidance had his heart set on travelling to Boston and working for General Electric. He was having difficulty in securing work in Boston. So I asked him how he was networking and suggested that networking could happen anywhere. The following week he called me, elated, and said that he had been offered an exciting job while at an under-12 football match. He had gone along to support his little brother and on the sideline he met a South African man. They got chatting and it emerged that the man ran a successful energy company in South Africa. They exchanged contact details and the unemployed graduate followed up with emails expressing interest in the project. Within a week, he was offered a great contract in South Africa! His friends couldn't believe it when they heard about his chance encounter.

Words like 'happenstance', 'serendipity' and 'synchronicity' all describe the wild card or luck factor that exists in career planning. Chance happenings, lucky encounters occur when you take a step into the world and take the initiative.

Reflect

Think back on your own career, how you chose your path and the subsequent jobs you had. Were there any occasions when you stumbled upon a job, met someone with a lead to a job, or were in the right place at the right time?

Share with your teen some of the chance happenings that helped shape your career.

While it is good to plan a route ahead with your child and help them identify goals that matter to them, it is also useful to prepare them to embrace the unexpected and remain open to opportunities. Your child will have to keep tacking and twisting depending on the opportunities that come their way or that they create. In the future world of work there will be little room for complacency.

TASK J: CHANCE HAPPENINGS

Get your teenager to read about their favourite celebrities, role models, sportspeople, entrepreneurs, musicians or inventors to see what role chance happenings and positive open responses had in their career journey. Perhaps they could talk about their findings, which might help them adopt a spirit of optimism and curiosity as they make plans for their own future.

Step 9 Key Points

- Change in life is inevitable. What is important is how we react to unwanted change or events.
- Make your teen aware of their resilience and help them to develop inner strength by building on their resilience.
- Helping your teen to be flexible, adaptable and versatile will help them harness the power of change to build career success.
- Pay attention to the value of chance happenings or luck. Help your teen to be alert to these and able to see and embrace opportunities as they arise.

As a parent, you can make your child aware of the gift of resilience. You can offer ways for them to enhance and develop their resilience and to cope with adversity. By doing this, you are preparing them for an ever-changing future world of work.

❖

MY CAREER

Colm Lynch
General Service Supervisor, Monaghan County Council
(Apprenticeship in Plumbing)

Monaghan County Council oversees and plans services such as arts and environment, road and transport, housing and planning, and water services for the county.

'If you do it wrong once it's not wrong until you do it the same way a second time. Take the advice nobody takes, "Listen to your parents." They mean the best for you.'

How did your career in plumbing/the county council begin?
I was leaving school and just wanted a trade (apprenticeship). When I was at school, rote learning did not suit me as I was more practical and wanted to use my hands in my career. Through FÁS [replaced by Solas and the Education and Training Boards (ETBs)], I did an apprenticeship in plumbing at Cork RTC, now known as CIT. I loved my apprenticeship and, unlike school, learning there was like second nature to me. Everything made sense. Following the apprenticeship, I worked with Monaghan County Council and I have been there since 1992.

Did you always want to do what you do now?

I entered the organisation as a plumber. While there, I observed many different types of people and the jobs they had. In particular, I was interested in the role of the general service supervisor. I aligned myself to him and I helped most of the time. In doing so, I learned a lot from him, not just about the trade, but an awful lot about people and the work we do in the organisation. Little did I know that that knowledge would stand to me later in life, as I have that job now. I'm lucky. Looking back, he was like an unofficial mentor to me.

What do you enjoy most about what you do now?

I enjoy working with people, motivating them and steering them in the right direction. I like to use my emotional intelligence with the people around me. I like to gauge and read people in relation to situations and respond appropriately. In that way, I can maximise the output of the people around me. I also enjoy meeting new people and working with them, which happens regularly in this job.

What is the toughest thing about your job?

Meeting the ever-changing standards of health and safety.

What motivates you?

If someone comes to me with a problem – for example, a house with no electrics or a lack of water – I like to meet that challenge and address that problem. I am motivated too by the fact that proper road signage and the implementation of health and safety measures can save lives.

Who or what inspired you along the way?

I have had so many inspirations. My first inspiration was the

Scouts. As a teenager, I thrived on being given a task and completing the task in a group, e.g. setting up a campsite. My second source of inspiration was the Civil Defence. I gained a lot of knowledge there, such as emergency exercise planning, which I can apply to my working life today. More important, I made good friends in the Scouts and Civil Defence. One of my highlights in the Civil Defence was when I walked shoulder to shoulder with Arnold Schwarzenegger onto the pitch at Croke Park for the Special Olympics in 1992. I got to meet Andrea Corr and Bono there too.

My third source of inspiration was my involvement in Mountain Rescue. As second officer, I learned to co-ordinate rescue operations. I developed planning skills and learned techniques to rescue people from ravines and cliffs. Now I bring all these practical skills to my work, life and hobby (canoeing). They have really boosted my confidence.

What advice on getting started would you give young people who want a career in the same field?
Volunteer for organisations. Be prepared to start for nothing. You'll gain knowledge, which is priceless. You will gain friends for life along the way.

What has been the biggest lesson in your career to date?
My biggest lesson to date was learning to use my discretion. Knowing what knowledge to keep, what knowledge to give out at times, and what knowledge not to give. I had to learn to listen to my gut and use my intuition.

If you had a motto, what would it be?
Have the craic, work hard and have a laugh; today could be the last.

What advice would you give your 16-year-old self?
Don't be afraid to make mistakes, everybody does. The man who never made a mistake never made anything. If you do it wrong once it's not wrong until you do it the same way a second time. Take the advice nobody takes, 'Listen to your parents.' They mean the best for you.

❖

Abundance and Creativity

Do not talk about hard times/necessity [because] speaking of economic lack and limitation keeps people in the poorhouse financially.

CATHERINE PONDER

A career coaching book for parents of teenagers that failed to mention the effects of recession and economic hard times would be incomplete. In recent years, some of our young people have internalised negative messages about the economy and the labour market and have simply given up. They wonder what is the point of being motivated and forming goals and plans.

In Step 10 you will:

- Become aware of limiting thoughts and how they could negatively influence career choices
- Become aware of ways that your teen can take more responsibility for creating abundance and taking charge of their own success
- Realise the negative effect an attitude of scarcity can have
- Realise the significance of opening the mind to creativity
- Learn techniques that will help reduce stress in your teen
- Be introduced to proven ways to stimulate creativity both in yourself and in your teen.

Parenting expert Professor Matt Sanders emphasises the importance of positive parenting during a recession: 'While the recession is putting families under financial pressure, parents need to "insulate their children" against the worst effects. ... In times of stress, parents have to step up to the plate to make sure their children are not damaged by the process.' He says that the challenge is to maintain a sense of optimism ('Don't blame the parents, help them', *Irish Times*, 7 June 2011).

You can help your teen avoid apathy by encouraging a positive outlook or a 'glass half full' mentality. You can help them take responsibility for themselves by coaching them to be in the driver's seat of their own lives rather than being passive passengers. Although not always mentioned in career planning, belief in **abundance and creativity** is crucial to enhancing our experience of life and work.

International motivational speaker Anthony Robbins says that true wealth is an emotion: it's a sense of absolute abundance. *Abundance* can be a feeling of riches, opportunity and plenty. It can come from appreciating art, walking in a park, appreciating health, family and friends, or feeling that business will pick up. In other words, the glass is more than half full, it is actually overflowing! *Limitation* is the other side of the coin. Limitation focuses on a lack of jobs, opportunities, resources, facilities and talent. It's a 'glass half empty' outlook. Focusing on limitations puts a firm lid on a teen's potential. Let's look at how limitation might be showing up in your child's thinking and how it can be replaced by an attitude of abundance.

Limitation

Messages of *limitation* tell us that there aren't enough resources in the world. These messages really block our access to abundance and are often considered by adults and teens as absolute truths. Limitation can be found in family messages such as:

- 'No one in our family will ever get into medical school.'
- 'This family will follow the safe, permanent, pensionable route; entrepreneurship is way too risky for us.'

There can also be messages about our genetics and gender.

I had a young female client who was unemployed for some time and isolated at home with her pet dog. We looked at her interests. From a young age, she was interested in motorbikes and had a keen aptitude for woodwork and construction studies. At school, she was the best in her class at these subjects; however, she felt she had to downplay her abilities in front of the boys and she chose to deliberately let her talents slide.

All too often, I meet young women who are talented in maths, science and engineering and yet they are dissuaded from following these paths by messages and stereotyping that indicate that these are subjects for men. Equally, some boys encounter resistance in areas such as fashion design, hairdressing and cooking because of some of the messages that surround those careers.

We also receive messages of limitation from school, our community, our religion and our society. These messages could be, 'No one in our community could do that' or 'That's unheard of for someone from X.' Some teenagers may think that universities such as UCD and Trinity are only for people from Dublin 4 or from fee-paying schools. Believing these messages can prevent them getting ahead. Equally, some teens have negative views of Post Leaving Cert courses and institutes of technology and as a result, they deny themselves the chance to develop solid, practical, technical skills. If our teens were aware of the falseness of these messages, perhaps they wouldn't fall victim to them and allow them to curb their fulfilment in life.

- When you were growing up, what were the messages you received about your family, school, community, religion and society?
- How did they influence your career choice?
- What impact did they have on you?
- What messages would you like to rewrite for future generations?

Make a conscious effort not to give messages of limitation in your home. As limitations arise, challenge them by looking for evidence of their truth. For example, 'Engineering is not for girls.' Ask, 'Is that true?' Find out how many women are studying engineering. Have a conversation with a female engineer. If you find that there are far fewer women engineers than men, think about what is preventing women becoming engineers.

Some adults fail to see the value of apprenticeships and of developing a trade or practical skills. They fail to see the openings in agriculture, horticulture, forestry, food production and some of the service industries. These areas are just as valuable as those for which you need a university qualification and they are needed throughout the world.

Excuses and Blame

Another area that blocks abundance and success in young people is the belief that success is out of their hands and lies in the hands of others. Some teens tend to make excuses and blame others for their lack of progress: teachers, parents, school, friends, where they live, the economy and even the weather. Here are some of the comments I have encountered:

- 'It's the teacher's fault – his classes are really boring and I can't be bothered studying.'
- 'If only my parents were cooler, life would be different!'
- 'It's just this school – if I were at another school I'd concentrate better.'
- 'Because of my physical or learning disability, I won't do well in life.'

These kinds of comment depict a situation wherein young people feel they have no choice and that they cannot access their power. But they can adopt an approach to life that helps them identify what is within their power to change, and take steps to changing it by *focusing on what they can control.* Difficult times mean that we are faced with the challenge of finding new ways to do things and of creating our own opportunities.

Tip! Focus on what You can Control

Focusing on what you can control is a concept from Stephen Covey's book, *The 7 Habits of Highly Effective People.* Covey advocates focusing on what we can change or influence, rather than on what we cannot. He describes two circles: our circle of concern and our circle of influence. A simplified version is shown below.

- There are many things that concern or impact on us. In the context of parenting a teen, their school and career choices, what they do and how they do it are of huge concern.
- Within that category, there is a smaller group of things that we can actually do something about; we have some control or influence over them. Examples might be the school they go to, whether or not they can go to university, house/home rules, etc.
- If, in any situation, we focus on what concerns us but we cannot control or change it, we will experience a lot of frustration or anger or stress. We can swim around in these negative emotions but still will not be able to do anything to change or influence things.
- If we focus on what we *can* influence, we are more likely to be able to move beyond the stress and negativity.
- Imagine a cup and saucer. Think of the **saucer** as all the things that concern us, but over which we have no control, for example the points our children get in their Leaving Cert; how much focus they put on their schoolwork; their taste in music.
- The **cup** is full of the things we *can* control or influence, for example the environment we provide at home to facilitate our teen's study; being a role model for them; communicating positively with them.

In any situation, ask yourself, 'Is this in the cup or on the saucer? Is this something I can do something about or not?' If not, what elements have you control over? Parent coach Marian Byrne says that you always have control over yourself and how you choose to respond.

I had a client from Dublin who had ADHD (attention deficit hyperactivity disorder), which made it difficult for him to focus and study. He blamed his ADHD for everything and felt that because of it, there was no point in studying. His parents and teachers could see his potential and encouraged him to apply himself. He said they were nagging him. No study environment seemed right for him and yet he wanted to go to university. He gave all his power away to his ADHD and didn't get his first choice of courses after the Leaving Cert, which caused him great disappointment.

This reaction contrasted with another male client who also had ADHD, dyspraxia and dyslexia. He suffered from constant anxiety and fear of failure. His anxiety was fuelled by large amounts of Red Bull. He proactively took steps to reduce the impact of his ADHD and anxiety because he wanted to get a qualification that would lead to a meaningful job. After school, he did a Post Leaving Cert course in Childcare Studies. Initially, he felt awkward as he was the only guy in the class and was surrounded by women. Nevertheless, he soon realised that he really wanted to work with children with special needs as he felt he could personally connect with and help them.

In order to succeed he first organised his study habits by studying early in the evening, using mind maps and not leaving assignments to the last minute. Second, he really tried to focus in class by listening carefully. This alone reduced his anxiety about tests and assignments. Third, he began to look after his health and significantly reduced his intake of Red Bull. In addition, he took up martial arts to practise discipline and to focus his mind. Overall, his grades began to improve along with his experience of learning. During work experience, he impressed an employer so much that he was offered a job when he finished the course.

Today, he loves his role as special needs assistant in a secondary school for kids with special needs and disabilities. He says, 'The kids love me and I love them and it doesn't feel like work at all. I love jumping out of bed in the morning. I have come a long way.'

Reflect

Are you at the mercy of events or do you proactively take steps to produce positive events/results in your working life or home life? Which side is your teen on?

List three ways in which you could create more choice, access more resources and gain more results in your own life.

1. _____
2. _____
3. _____

Name three ways in which your teen could take more responsibility and feel that they have control over their career path and choices.

1. _____
2. _____
3. _____

Scarcity Versus Abundance

Scarcity is the belief that there is not enough of something to go around: a lack of jobs, college places, diminishing funding and limited opportunities.

Our minds can stop us following our dreams by focusing on lack and scarcity – on what there is not, or on what we don't have. Do any of the following sound familiar?

- 'I won't get the points I need.'
- 'There are not enough college places.'
- 'It's impossible to make money in the arts.'
- 'My luck won't last.'
- 'There aren't enough opportunities in Ireland.'
- 'It will all go wrong.'

Much of the media focus on lack: mass unemployment, bankruptcy, closures, mortgage arrears, government cutbacks, slow business and emigration. While this may be part of the reality around us, we can decide to focus on abundance rather than on scarcity. When we adopt an attitude of **abundance**, we focus on a future full of openings and opportunities. Within each of us, there are unlimited ideas, talent and possibilities.

Abundance is linked to positivity. Studies show that in order to function normally in our working and personal lives we need to experience three positive thoughts to every negative thought. This means that when we are feeling disappointed and disillusioned, it is important that we make a conscious effort to see opportunities and note the good things in our lives. This makes us more resilient and better able to cope with life's difficulties.

Each day, new jobs are created, new business ideas are launched, songs are written, books published, movies released and inventions made. Bearing this in mind – and given the backdrop of our media – it is important that the flow of abundance and creative thinking is not cut off in our young people. If young people feel overwhelmed by the effects of recession and hard times, their ability to come up with solutions, innovations and creative ideas for business, research and development is stifled.

The inventors of YouTube were three young guys who thought, 'Wouldn't it be great if someone invented a website where people could upload and share video clips?' Within eighteen months, they had built a $1.65 billion company. The inventor of Facebook was a 19-year-old Harvard student who wanted to create an online version of student photo books. This idea spread into a global social networking site. Here in Ireland, one hub of recent creativity has been Ballyfermot College of Further Education, which was instrumental in the production of acclaimed films and animations such as *Avatar, Granny O'Grimm* and the Oscar-nominated *Secret of Kells*.

When the mind is open to abundant thinking and when the creative juices are flowing, opportunities are created. Then we are free to come up with answers to 'Wouldn't it be great if ...?', and to see gaps in the market.

Reflect

In what ways could you feed your mind and body with rich ideas (e.g. books, beauty, music, art, scenery, meditation, good food, prayer, comedy, positive thinking, sport)?

1. _____
2. _____
3. _____

In what ways could your teen feed themselves with rich ideas?

1. _____

2. _____

3. _____

- -

Step 10 Key Points

- Focusing on limitation and scarcity can result in apathy, frustration and helplessness.
- By using the 'circle of concern', your teen can reduce stress and focus on what is within their power to change.
- By focusing on what they can control, your teen can learn to take responsibility for their own lives and stop blaming others.
- Embrace abundance and find ways to unleash your and your teen's creativity. Notice how quickly new opportunities and possibilities present themselves as a result.

Well done! As a parent career coaching your teen, you are now on the front foot in a rapidly changing work world. Use these techniques to help your teen look at the world in a positive light and navigate their own career journey with hope and confidence!

❖

MY CAREER

Jenny Murphy
Award-winning Florist
www.flowersbymoira.ie

Winner of the Gold Medal at the 2012 Chelsea Flower Show and the coveted title of Florist of the Year 2012, Jenny has competed internationally, most recently in Singapore in

2014. Jenny works with her mother at Flowers by Moira in Dunshaughlin, Co. Meath.

'I can and I will!'

How did your career in floristry begin?
I grew up around and spent my holidays working in my mother's shop, Flowers by Moira. I never thought for one moment that I would end up working there. Initially, I thought I would become a vet, but I didn't get the points and went on to study a BSc in Marketing instead, as I had an interest in business. A trip to Australia and working in a florist's there cemented my desire to get into the flower business. I realised how much I loved weddings and event work along with customer interaction and creativity. I was really inspired by the relationship and interaction between shape, form and colours.

What do you enjoy most about what you do now?
I love the design element of working with flowers. My favourite time is when I am working late at night without distraction. The phones are quiet and I am in the zone where I can focus and experiment and take the time to explore for an event or wedding. I also love the way the seasons keep the job fresh. There is an excitement about the particular flowers, selection, colour and feeling of each season. When I'm at international flower trade shows, I'm a bit like a kid in a sweet shop. Flowers bring me joy. I am committed to feeding my inspiration and I go on courses and attend workshops in order to update my skills.

What is the toughest thing about your job?
Managing timelines. Flowers are perishable and need to look

fresh and vibrant for an event. Projects can take longer than you anticipate. Flowers need to arrive from Holland on a Wednesday and Thursday and that can leave time tight for Saturday weddings. I like my displays to be perfect and I care about my customers. I want each event or wedding to have that 'wow factor'. Delivering excellence and getting it right within the timeframe is a tricky balancing act.

What motivates you?
Serving my clients and making sure my product is right for them. It is important for me to uphold the name and reputation of Flowers by Moira. In particular, I am very motivated when it comes to learning and developing my craft. I love to explore new techniques and to look further afield to international designers and learn from them too.

Who or what inspired you along the way?
My mother has been my main source of inspiration. She has instilled in me a good work ethic, taught me to value learning and has encouraged my education. I am continuing her business, her connections and her relationships. Mum helped me blossom.

What advice on getting started would you give young people who want a career in the same field?
Go and do it. Try it out. Get as much experience as you can. Floristry is not brain surgery. Enjoy and progress with it.

What has been the biggest lesson in your career to date?
'Every day is a school day.' That runs through everything in my career.

If you had a motto, what would it be?

'I can and I will!' I have faith in my ability. Of course, I had some self-doubt when entering the competitions in Chelsea and in Singapore. Overall, I have had faith in my abilities and have said yes to every opportunity. I focused on winning gold in Chelsea and I put my mind to it. Today, I am wearing a bracelet and necklace by an Irish designer with the affirmation 'success'.

What advice would you give your 16-year-old self?

Believe in yourself and go for it!

A Final Optimistic Note!

I am the master of my fate:
I am the captain of my soul.

WILLIAM ERNEST HENLEY, 'INVICTUS'

Every parent wants what is best for his or her child and you are your teen's head coach. We are all naturally wired to listen to and feed the negative voice in our heads. We need to reprogramme ourselves into thinking positively and encouraging our young people to do the same. I am not advocating a rose-tinted view of the world or a Pollyanna approach to life. At times, a negative voice has a purpose and can serve as a form of self-protection for your child. Generally, however, if your child faces times when things do not go as planned, teach them to use positive self-talk. This will help them to acknowledge that even though things did not go as planned, they did their best and they will be able to seek other routes which will get them to where they want to be in the end.

As a parent, your most important task is to train your child to seek their own inner guidance and wisdom. It is not your job to have all the answers. They need to learn from their own experiences. You can support them as they discover their preferences and as they become who they are truly meant to be in this world. That means at time you may have to bite your tongue and stay out of their way or remain silent about your worries our concerns as they discover what is wrong or right for themselves. If as a parent you don't tell them what to do or what to choose and don't impose your preferences on them, then later in life they cannot blame you for their choices. That doesn't mean that you take no interest in them and remain a passive observer. Of course you offer stability and act as a touchstone for endless conversations about choices. In conversations, it is more beneficial and evokes a better response if you appeal to their wiser side and speak to them as if they are more mature than they already are.

If you implement even a few of the tips in this book, you will be better able to have an open dialogue with your teen and help them discover their sense of purpose. They will develop a keener sense of their own competence and will have more confidence in their ability to seek opportunities. This process will strengthen their understanding of who they are and this will sustain them in times of uncertainty.

Your teen may take a longer route to their dream career; they may do a one-year Post Leaving Cert (PLC) course or an access course. They may begin with an apprenticeship and work their way up the ladder by engaging in part-time learning. They may take a year out to volunteer and, in the process, learn more about themselves and how they interact with the world around them. They may well work for a few years and then decide to go to college as a mature student. They may even change careers along the way. All in all, it is important to realise that your teen is unique and that their journey need not follow a linear path.

> You can inspire your child to discover the star within, and your encouragement and open dialogue will help them along the way to a shining, happy, prosperous future!

Below is a summary of what you can do to help your teenager make good career choices.

1. **Think about ways to build confidence** and help your teenager embark confidently on their career path.

2. **Think about your own journey and encourage others** such as family, friends and godparents to share their career experiences with your teen.

3. **Encourage the development of passions.** Explore your teen's passions, interests, skills, values and personality. Encourage hobbies and interests beyond socialising. Take the time to get to know what matters most to your teen, and find common ground.

4. **Explore dreams.** Take time to discuss what your teen's ideal life might be like. Once you and your teenager begin to talk about their dreams, their motivation will increase naturally.

5. **Try out the world of work.** Keep career planning and exploration at the forefront of your mind. Encourage your child to find work experience, shadowing and volunteering.

6. **Tap into and widen your networks** when possible in order to introduce your teen to people and opportunities that are in line with their interests and that can inspire and inform them. See page 127 for tips on creating that elevator pitch for networking. Suggest to your teenager that they learn from experts and model themselves on successful people. Where possible, seek mentors.

7. **Keep informed.** Be aware of what employers want and inform your teenager about the importance of transferable skills. Keep abreast of the changing world of work and be aware of the importance of your teen leading their career. Refer to the websites in Further Resources at the end of the book for information on different sectors.

8. **Create school, college and training connections.** Attend meetings and information sessions with your teen's career guidance counsellor and teachers. Whenever possible, take time to visit colleges, universities and training centres. Stay informed

about college open days and refer to the Central Applications Office (CAO) and the Universities and Colleges Admissions Service (UCAS) websites for information on applications to Irish and UK colleges. Guidance counsellors are available at school for one-to-one help and advice. Most schools have career classes and a careers library. Guidance counsellors often organise careers evenings and mock interviews, information evenings on subject choice and CAO applications, and trips to open days and the higher options fairs. I would urge you to use the expertise of the guidance counsellor in your child's school and talk to them at parent/teacher meetings.

Above All!

Enjoy the journey you are taking with your teenager. You can play a key role in helping your child achieve their dreams. Some dreams take longer than others to unfold and some career paths emerge as your teenager's personality develops. Life is often understood better in hindsight, so you are best placed to positively encourage your teenager make a succession of forward steps. Help them to develop a good attitude – to value hard work and commitment, develop good communication and decision-making skills and learn from others. Having the right attitude cultivates success.

Your teenager will have many voices calling them in every direction and the challenge is to listen to that voice that speaks of service, of good and of happiness. This voice will point them towards the work that they really need to do and which the world needs to have done.

Where your talents and the needs of the world cross; there lies your vocation. (Aristotle)

Above all, let your teen listen to their heart to determine their direction in life. As I wish you and your teen the best of luck, I want to leave you with one more story:

The Lesson: Advice from a Veteran Trapeze Artist
The sage was with some of his friends when he witnessed an old lady training her grandson for the trapeze. The boy made three or four futile efforts to get over the bar. Then the old lady said, 'Son, if you throw your heart over the bars, your body will follow.' The sage commented, 'She's teaching a fundamental lesson, not so much about the trapeze as about life. It's the heart that determines the direction of life.'

MY CAREER

Paul Campbell
Focus Factory Manager
Medical Device Manufacturer, Athlone, Co. Westmeath

The company I work for creates medical devices and medical supplies, which serve healthcare needs in hospitals, long-term care, doctors' offices and homes. It is an international company located in seventy different countries.

'Don't be afraid to take risks. It will work out. If you have a burning desire, follow it through, trust your gut. If you fail, don't take it personally. Figure out why you failed, dust yourself off, and try again with a different approach or technique.'

How did your career in engineering begin?

I have worked in manufacturing for over twenty years. It started with me picking a university course that seemed to fit with my general engineering aptitude. Upon graduating, an opportunity to travel to Japan came up and I went for it. I worked there in the automotive field with Sumitomo for three years. At 21 years of age, I was fortunate to gain experience in Sumitomo, as they were world leaders in progressive manufacturing techniques. This experience shaped who I am today. Sumitomo taught me the value of teamwork and the 'Five Whys?' (What's the problem? Why did it happen? Why did that occur?, etc.) in order to identify root causes. I learned the basis of lean manufacturing. Sumitomo then invited me to establish a plant in the USA and I moved there for ten years. I then returned to Ireland and all my previous experience got me into medical device manufacturing.

Did you always want to do what you do now?

I originally wanted to be an accountant as I was good with numbers. My guidance counsellor at school pointed out that, while I was good with numbers, I was also practical and technical, and steered me towards engineering. Initially, I started out as an engineer in manufacturing. However, my position as manager evolved as I grew. Along the way, I acted as a link and a cultural bridge between the USA and Japan for Sumitomo. This gave me a lot of experience dealing with cultures and managing people. I took a leap of faith, embraced managerial opportunities, and completed an MBA. Today, I am less about engineering and more about leading four hundred people in manufacturing.

What do you enjoy most about what you do now?
I now manage a large manufacturing team and I most enjoy working with them to make things better. I love the team that I have working for me. The best days are when the team realise that they have made an improvement that will make their job easier and better. Overall, I enjoy going in every day and facing challenges. I thrive on being able to deal with ambiguity and having to rely on my value system to make the right decision.

What is the toughest thing about your job?
The toughest thing about my job is helping people to manage change. It can be a challenge to get people to buy into and to agree to changes. It can be a challenge to help people deal with the uncertainty that comes with change. Of course, there are things outside our control too, such as accidents. It can also be a challenge to create more of a positive culture and to eradicate blame.

What motivates you?
I am motivated when I'm successful at getting people to agree to try something new, to agree to change and to see things differently.

Who or what inspired you along the way?
My parents inspired me to make education an important part of life and taught me that with hard work, you will achieve. My Japanese manager, Mr Morai, had a profound influence on me. Mr Morai was a great manager and he knew how to motivate me. I observed his excellent leadership qualities, how he listened to everyone, respected opinions and valued

his team. He always made informed decisions; sometimes they were tough, as they were based on his principles. He taught me how to bring a sense of perspective to the job. In addition, I learned how to weigh up pros and cons and to be realistic while creating a vision.

What advice on getting started would you give young people who want a career in the same field?

You have to be confident. Be aware of your communication styles. Work on your communication skills. Communication skills are hugely important and span from day-to-day matters to leadership. Concentrate on opportunities, there are many opportunities here and abroad. Ireland is a great country in which to get an education and you can travel the world with it. Be optimistic, confident, work hard, have fun and you will enjoy great things.

What has been the biggest lesson in your career to date?

If you want it bad enough, you will get it. Along the way, I have learned the value of perseverance in my career.

If you had a motto, what would it be?

Don't be afraid to take risks. It will work out. If you have a burning desire, follow it through, trust your gut. If you fail, don't take it personally. Figure out why you failed, dust yourself off, and try again with a different approach or technique.

What advice would you give your 16-year-old self?

First, get an education, or develop skills. They will open many doors. Take chances. Say 'yes' to opportunities (at 16, I never planned to live and work in Japan or the States). Make the most of opportunities when they come your way. Then, follow your gut instinct and see where it brings you. It is an exciting journey and the destination unfolds as you grow as a person. Good luck!

❖

Appendix 1

Additional Questions to Ask in an Informational Interview

1. What is your favourite part of your job?
2. What is your least favourite part of your job?
3. What surprised you the most when you started working in this field?
4. How do you see this industry developing in the future? How is your industry changing?
5. What are employers typically looking for when hiring people in this line of work?
6. My background and experience is ...; or I am considering specialising in .... How does that compare with employers' expectations when hiring in this industry?
7. May I have your business card?
8. Is there anyone else I might talk to about this? May I use your name when I contact that person?

See more at www.careerchoiceguide.com/informational-interview-questions.html

Appendix 2

Senior Cycle Education and Applying to College

Upper secondary-level education is usually taken by students between the ages of 15 and 18. The programme of study can take between two and three years. The difference in duration depends on whether or not a student chooses to do Transition Year. This is an optional programme between the Junior Certificate and the Leaving Certificate.

Transition Year offers a wide range of personal, social development and work-related experiences. When it is well co-ordinated, students mature, grow, develop self-awareness, skills and get a better sense of appropriate career choices through work experience. After Transition Year, students go on to the two-year Leaving Cert Programme.

Most students take the **Leaving Cert** (established) which leads to the traditional Leaving Cert exam after two years. Some students take the **Leaving Cert Vocational Programme** (LCVP), which emphasises enterprise education and preparation for the world of work. Some students prefer to follow a less academic, more self-contained programme that is learner-centred and pre-vocational in nature. This is the **Leaving Cert Applied** (LCA).

At Leaving Certificate level, established Leaving Cert/LCVP subjects are offered with different variations according to the schools. The LCA offers traditional subjects through nine courses. Visit the National Council for Curriculum and Assessment (NCCA) website (www.ncca.ie) for further details.

Communicate with your school. Most guidance counsellors in schools have information evenings for parents on subject choices and on the senior cycle programmes. Where guidance is provided in schools, guidance counsellors offer workshops and one-to-one support in subject choices and decision-making.

The Points System

Specific points are allocated for each grade your teen gets in the Leaving Cert. More points are awarded for the Higher Level subjects. Entry to college courses is awarded on the basis of a points system. Points change according to supply and demand; they vary each year and can go up or down. Courses will require a certain number of 'entry points'. Most colleges count the grades from the student's best six subjects. In the past, many students dropped down to Pass maths for this reason. Throughout the country, performance in maths dropped and as a result, and in order to emphasise the importance of maths to the economy, bonus points were awarded to maths. The table below illustrates point allocation.

HOW POINTS ARE CALCULATED

Note: The scores from the best six subjects are used to calculate points.

Marks	Grade	Points for Higher Level	Points for Ordinary Level	Points for Foundation Maths
90–100	A1	100	60	20
85–89	A2	90	50	15
80–84	B1	85	45	10
75–79	B2	80	40	5
70–74	B3	75	35	
65–69	C1	70	30	
60–64	C2	65	25	
55–59	C3	60	20	
50–54	D1	55	15	
45–49	D2	50	10	
40–44	D3	45	5	
Link Modules	Distinction	70		
Link Modules	Merit	50		
Link Modules	Pass	30		

A new CAO points system for college entry is set to be introduced for the Leaving Certificate students of 2017. It aims to reward the students sitting the higher level who narrowly miss a pass (30–39%) on an honours paper. A new grading scale will be introduced in place of the 14 different bands from A1 to NG (no grade). The plan is for eight bands: H1–H8 at higher level, and O1–O8 at ordinary level.

The new scales are designed to allow for greater distinctions between CAO applicants and to minimise the random selection that can happen under the current system.

It is anticipated that colleges will design courses with fewer and wider entry routes to allow for a common first year. Common first years in science or engineering will allow students to sample subjects and specialise after their first year. (See Katherine Donnelly, 'Changes to CAO points system on the cards for 2017 exams', *Irish Independent*, 27 April 2015.)

It is important to note that if your teen is disappointed with their points score, they could do a PLC, access course or an apprenticeship, or consider going to college as a mature student at age 23+, when points are not the only criteria. There are also graduate entry programmes to medicine and other disciplines that require high points. Some universities offer graduates a conversion master's that allows students to achieve their career goals over a longer time period.

For example, the University of Limerick offers a master's in Occupational Therapy to graduates of other disciplines with relevant experience. This allows students who didn't achieve the required points the first time around to get into occupational therapy at a later stage. It is worth exploring graduate entry routes where appropriate, especially in the case of primary teaching.

Not everyone needs to go to college and a college degree is not a prerequisite for success. The interviews in this book show that there are plenty of people who follow vocational paths, trades or the defence forces and achieve great success.

What are the Different Levels of Study?

The National Framework of Qualifications (NFQ) is used to classify and compare qualifications. The NFQ is a system of ten levels (see the full-colour diagram of levels on www.nfq.ie). Each level corresponds to a competence and skill level associated with each qualification. The ones that we are familiar with at second level are the Junior and Leaving Certificates and these are awarded by the State Examinations Commission. Further education and training qualifications are awarded by Quality and Qualifications Ireland (QQI). FETAC awards (further education qualifications and training) are now made by Solas and the Education and Training Boards (ETBs) (formerly VECs and FÁS).

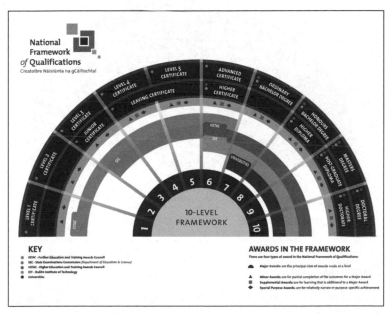

Higher education and training qualifications may be awarded by QQI, the institutes of technology, the Royal College of Surgeons in Ireland or the universities. The system allows for progression through the levels and some people may take a more scenic route to higher education. Many of the levels lead to employment upon completion. The QQI website (www.qqi.ie) is an excellent source of information.

There is a European and global equivalences framework, which allows people to move from country to country with their qualifications. The European Framework has eight levels, while

Ireland has ten levels (see www.qqi.ie). The QQI offers a qualification advice service which translates Irish qualifications to those in other countries. This service offers greater mobility and widens the platform of opportunity for people holding Irish qualifications.

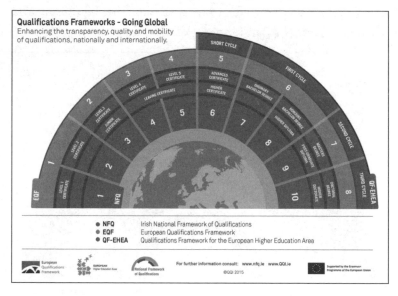

The CAO

Nowadays, most students in sixth year apply online to the Central Applications Office (CAO) on www.cao.ie. Before doing this, it is important to consult the CAO handbook for the correct course code, title and contact details. This can be downloaded in a PDF format. Go through this handbook with your teen when they are making choices. Consult college websites for admission requirements, course details, subjects and career opportunities. Most schools have a guidance counsellor. Guidance counsellors are qualified in careers counselling and they are available to your teen for careers advice. Many guidance counsellors are qualified in psychometric testing, which means that they can administer tests that indicate suitable preferences and aptitudes. Encourage your teen to make an appointment. Some guidance counsellors offer information evenings for parents explaining the CAO system and other options. It is important not to miss these opportunities in order to develop an awareness of the systems and to get your queries answered.

The CAO application process can be stressful for students and parents. Here are a few tips that can ensure you do it effectively and with as little stress as possible:

- Apply early and online at www.cao.ie. If you apply by the early deadline of 5.15 p.m. on 20 January you pay a discounted rate of €25. The normal application fee is €40 and the cut-off date is 5.15 p.m. on 1 February. (*Note:* these dates may vary year to year.)

- Keep in mind that sometimes there is a CAO rush and the system can get over-loaded, so apply early. Early application helps minimise last-minute errors.

- Consider the entry requirements needed. Some courses require a particular grade in honours maths, a certain science subject or a third language. Check out the entry requirements at www.cao.ie, Qualifax (www.qualifax.ie), Careers Portal (www.careersportal.ie) or college websites.

- Think carefully about your choices. What were your impressions of a course or college during an open day or visit? The atmosphere and the environment in which your teen will be learning are important. Consider going to an open day with your teen. Many colleges hold open days on Saturdays so that students can attend without missing school. An open day offers a great opportunity to travel with your son or daughter and attend the day as a shared experience. College involves a huge investment of your money and resources and requires a large commitment on everybody's part. You are entitled to ask questions on a visit in order to make sure that your teen makes the best choice. Bear in mind that if you as a parent go to an open day you may incur travel costs.

- Conduct informational interviews with people who have pursued the career you are considering. If, for example, you are interested in social work, speak to a social worker and ask them about the pros and cons of their job. If at all possible, work shadow a person in your desired field.

- Talk to students who are studying the courses you are interested in. In particular, talk to third- or final-year students and get a sense of the level of commitment required and the content involved. Approach the college directly. Speak to the heads of department and lecturers about the course content and prospects after graduation. Generally, they will be happy to assist you.

- Most colleges and universities have a record of 'graduate destinations'. Call the admissions or careers service and find out what previous graduates went on to do. What are the general employment prospects for those who studied the course you are interested in? Does your undergraduate degree or course require a postgraduate qualification in order to improve career possibilities? As a parent, you will be making a huge investment of your resources; therefore, it would be beneficial to look at future prospects.

- Closely examine the course prospectus. See if your course allows for a year of study abroad. A second language and international experience are greatly valued by employers. Check also to see if your course involves work experience. Having relevant work experience enhances your future job prospects.

- Consider each of your twenty choices wisely. Use all of your choices: ten choices at Level 8, and ten choices at Levels 6 and 7. Remember, you can always climb the ladder of qualifications. (Level 8 is an honours degree, Level 7 a general or ordinary-

level degree, and Level 6 a two-year higher certificate course.)
See www.qqi.ie for an explanation of the system.

- Include some courses with lower points. Each year, thousands
of students with 500 points receive no offers at all!

- Keep in mind that some courses have 'restricted application'.
These courses involve assessments in March or April. For
example, art and design courses involve portfolio evaluations
and music degrees require music tests. Applications to nursing
for mature students are also restricted and involve an aptitude
test. Medicine is also restricted and requires a Health Professions
Admissions Test (HPAT).

- Place all your courses in your genuine order of preference. It
is a **major** mistake to base your choices solely on the points of
previous years or your expected grades. In the CAO system,
you get what you ask for. Again, the most important thing
is to **fill out your form in order of your preference**. Fill it
out according to what you really want to do, not according to
points.

- Refer to the 'Alert List' on the CAO site. This list shows courses
that have been either added to or removed from the CAO
handbook.

- Finally, don't panic. You have the opportunity to correct or
amend your application between 5 February and 1 March if
you want to include a re-restricted course. There is a 'change of
mind' facility for 'normal applications' from 5 May to 1 July. So
you have plenty of opportunities to rethink your choices and
make changes.

SUSI: Student Universal Support Ireland

SUSI is an important resource for parents. It offers grants
and assistance, and application is made online. Refer to www.
studentfinance.ie to check for eligibility and to make an application.

Grant applications can be made from the end of April to the beginning of May.

- Undergraduate students who meet certain criteria (means tested) and secure a place on an approved course may receive both the maintenance and fee portions of the student grant.
- Post Leaving Cert (PLC) students who meet certain criteria and are on an approved course are eligible to receive only the maintenance portion of the student grant.

Please refer to www.susi.ie to familiarise yourself with conditions of eligibility.

Helpline: Support for Parents and Students

August is a crucial time for both parents and Leaving Cert students. Many parents and students have lots of concerns and questions at this time. However, professional help is near at hand after the Leaving Certificate results are out and around the time of the CAO. At this time of year, a helpline (1800 265 165) is provided courtesy of the National Parents' Council in association with the *Irish Independent*, Eircom and the Department of Education and Skills (DES). The Institute of Guidance Counsellors (IGC) is employed to provide qualified guidance counsellors to give advice and support to parents and students. At this time of year many guidance counsellors are available when the CAO offers come out and to discuss other options too. See the National Parents' Council for further details (www.npcpp.ie).

Post Leaving Cert Courses (PLCs)

A PLC course can be an excellent bridge between secondary school and third-level education or a stand-alone qualification. PLCs are offered at local level throughout the country under the aegis of the

ETBs. ETBs are made up of former VECs and former FÁS Training Centres under Solas. ETBs offer further education and training opportunities as well as apprenticeships. PLCs are available to students who have completed the Leaving Cert. The qualification is usually placed at QQI Levels 5 and 6 and is recognised by colleges and employers.

PLCs comprise eight modules and include work experience. Assessments involve assignments, projects, research and examinations. The Qualifax website offers a list of PLC courses at both national and county level; see www.qualifax.ie. Under the course listing in the PLC section, you will see the variety of courses available, including sports, art, pre-nursing, travel and tourism, hairdressing and so on.

PLCs offer grants that are means tested by SUSI (see www. studentfinance.ie). If you are above the income threshold and don't qualify for a grant they tend to cost a lot less than the registration fee for a CAO course. As PLCs are widely available, taking a PLC course will allow your teen to live at home and commute. This reduces the costs of accommodation and living away from home.

The advantages of a PLC include links into third-level colleges. Certain courses on the CAO accept PLC with QQI Levels 5 and 6 under the Higher Education Links Scheme (HELS). So if your teen did not get the points required for a CAO course, this gives them a route in, depending on their results and module requirements. Check the CAO online system to see which institutions offer PLCs and to check the essential modules required. Some PLCs require an interview as part of the selection process.

PLCs are widely varied and some lead to full-time employment. They can also clarify career direction for teenagers or young adults who are unsure about what they want to do, or act as an alternative gap year. It is a safe way to try out a vocational area for fit before jumping into a four-year degree option.

Apply directly to your local ETB or further education college for a PLC. Keep in mind that certain PLCs are hugely popular. Before applying, visit open days at the colleges to get a sense of the course.

Repeating Leaving Cert

Repeat Leaving Cert options are available throughout the country. Some are available in ETBs and there are other private options. For many years, the Institute of Education, Dublin has been offering a Repeat Leaving Cert Programme. If your teen has met the matriculation requirements, e.g. the third language or Irish, there is no need to repeat that subject. This allows for more time to focus on getting higher points in other subjects. Use Google to explore your options and apply direct to your chosen college. Before you sign up, examine your motivation, your reasons for repeating, and the advantages of repeating the Leaving Cert.

UCAS

UCAS is the application system for colleges and universities in the UK (including Northern Ireland). It is different from the CAO system. It can act as a Plan B or insurance option to the CAO. In the UCAS system, you can apply for up to five courses. The system is based on 'Tariff points', as shown in the table.

COMPARISON OF LEAVING CERT AND UCAS TARIFF POINTS

Irish Leaving Cert		
Higher	Ordinary	UCAS tariff points
A1		90
A2		77
B1		71
B2		64
B3		58
C1		52
C2		45
C3	A1	39
D1		33
D2	A2	26
D3	B1	20
	B2	14
	B3	7

It is worth noting that the system may allow points for grades attained in music, drama and ballet; and it may also allow points and recognition for PLC courses and QQI qualifications. The application requires more information than the CAO, such as details of your educational history, predicted grades, employment so far, a personal statement and references.

The application deadline is 6 p.m. on 15 October for universities such as Oxford or Cambridge and most courses in medicine, veterinary medicine, science and dentistry. Many of these courses also require an admissions test. The UCAS website (www.ucas. com) has comprehensive details about requirements. Some courses also involve an interview selection process and sometimes an essay test.

The majority of courses have a 15 January deadline, although it is wise to apply as early as possible. Art and design courses have particular requirements, such as a portfolio, and 24 March is the deadline for these courses. In the UCAS system, the Personal Statement is of utmost importance as this is your chance to show course providers **why you want to study the course and why you would make a great student**. Putting time and consideration into this statement and making sure that you demonstrate your suitability for your chosen course makes all the difference to the selection process.

When planning ahead, bear in mind that many UK universities charge steep fees. Any EU student who is applying to Scotland for their primary degree is not eligible to pay fees. The NHS funds some courses in the health professions. Certain other courses are also funded. Check the universities in question to clarify fees and other information. The Student Loans Compnay (www.slc.co.uk) offers a low-interest loan to cover fees at third-level institutions throughout the UK. This loan is paid back when the student graduates, secures employment and earns more than £19,000 sterling. See www.ucas.com for further information.

The UCAS Clearing System, for places not yet filled, can be accessed after the Leaving Cert results are released.

Other Countries

Some Irish students consider studying abroad, and it can be advantageous to study subjects such as medicine and dentistry overseas. Some countries, such as Austria, Denmark, Luxembourg, Norway and Sweden, have no fees, while others have low fees. It is important to check with the country in question about their fee system. As each country has a different system, check the fees, living costs and the recognition of qualifications in order to make an informed decision. Also see www.studentfinance.ie to check for grant eligibility.

While at an Irish university, your teen could also take part in a **Erasmus** programme (European Community Action Scheme for Mobility of University Students). This is funded by a grant and allows students who have completed the first year of a degree/ diploma course to spend time in an EU university. Time spent abroad is viewed favourably by employers and also offers an opportunity to improve language skills. If you would like to explore applying to university in Europe, contact Eunicas (European University Central Application Support Service) at www.eunicas. ie. Also go to www.learnabroad.ie for more information.

Appendix 3

Third-level Scholarships in Ireland and Abroad

All universities and institutes of technology (ITs) offer their own scholarships. It is important to visit the institution's own website to get details of what is available there.

In addition, there is also the **Student Assistance Fund** for students who are experiencing financial hardship. The fund is administered on a confidential basis by the Higher Education Authority (HEA) on behalf of the Department of Education and Skills. Applications for this fund should be made to the disability/access officer in the student's institution. See www.studentfinance.ie for further details.

SUSI (Student Universal Support Ireland, www.susi.ie) offers student grants and assistance. Applications (online) can be made from the end of April to the beginning of May. Undergraduate students are eligible for both the maintenance and fee portions of the student grant; PLC students may receive only the maintenance portion of the grant. See www.studentfinance.ie to check for eligibility and to make an application.

Academic Achievement Entrance Scholarships

This is the main type of entrance scholarship available at universities and ITs. These scholarships are awarded to first-year students based on their points score in the Leaving Certificate: University College Dublin (560+ points); Dublin City University (550+); Dublin IT (500+ (specified courses)) and University College Cork

(500+ (specified courses)). Maynooth University offers entrance scholarships of €1,000 to each first year who achieves 525+ points. Other institutions offer other awards based on their own criteria and eligibility, for example:

- *University College Cork:* Quercus Talented Student's Programme – covers areas such as academia, active citizenship, creative and performing arts, innovation, entrepreneurship and sport
- *University of Limerick:* Paddy Dooley Rowing Club Scholarship.

Sports Scholarships

Most Irish third-level institutions offer sports scholarships, which offer a variety of perks such as tailored coaching, nutritional advice, financial supports, access to physiotherapy and sports psychologists, and reduced-cost accommodation. Successful candidates are often expected to make themselves available for selection for their institution's team(s). Some universities offer eligible elite athletes up to 60 CAO performance points.

Maynooth University, Dublin City University and University College Dublin offer limited places on undergraduate courses through their Elite Sportspersons Schemes, under which students' sporting achievements are taken into consideration alongside CAO performance.

These scholarships are referred to as sports scholarships, elite athlete scholarships or performance points scholarships. Visit each college website to find relevant information.

Artistic Scholarships

Trinity College Dublin, National University of Ireland Galway and University College Cork offer specific scholarships in the creative and performing arts field. Further information is available on the college websites.

Other Financial Scholarships

In an initiative to address disadvantage, the DES offers DEIS Bursaries to schools that fall into the Delivering Equality of Opportunity in Schools category. These awards are awarded automatically on the basis of Leaving Cert performance to those who match the criteria. In 2015, sixty bursaries will be made available.

In addition, there are eight bursaries available to students from DEIS schools who will pursue science, technology, engineering and mathematics (STEM). These are called the Ernest Walton STEM bursaries. Application should be made to Higher Education – Equity of Access, DES, Portlaoise Road, Tullamore, Co. Offaly.

All-Ireland Scholarships

The All-Ireland Scholarship Scheme was established in 2008 with a donation of €30 million from J.P. McManus. The scheme is administered by the DES. Up to 100 scholarships are made available in the Republic and 25 in Northern Ireland to those who meet the eligibility criteria. Candidates must be recognised as being from disadvantaged backgrounds. Selection is based on candidates' Leaving Cert results. No application is needed. See www.allirelandscholarships.com for more information.

Fund for Students with Disabilities

This fund aims to give students assistance, support and equipment where required in order to help them with their studies. Contact the institution's disability or access officer to discuss ways of getting the required support. See www.studentfinance.ie for further information.

Important note: Conditions and criteria for all scholarships can change from year to year, so it's important to check for current information.

Appendix 4

Disabilities and Specific Learning Difficulties

Forms of Support

If you are the parent of a teenager with a disability or a specific learning disorder such as dyspraxia, dyslexia or dyscalculia, it is important to seek out the supports that will help your teen achieve their dream. Support organisations that may be able to help your teen include:

- **AHEAD** (the Association for Higher Education Access and Disability) provides advice and support for students with disabilities who want to access higher education. They encourage full access to third-level education for students with disabilities. They also assist with employment after graduation. They provide excellent information on resources at www.ahead.ie and you can call them on 01 716 4396.
- **Disability Access Route in Education (DARE)** is an access route for students who want to go into higher education; it is a supplementary admissions scheme for students with a disability. See www.accesscollege.ie for further information. Strict deadlines apply under this scheme.
- **CAO** is the same for all students. However, students with a disability or specific learning difficulty are advised to tick the 'Med Box' on the first page. This box is used to advise colleges or universities that supports will be needed. See www.cao.ie.
- **Access/disability officers:** many third-level institutions have a disability officer who will work with individuals with disabilities to address their support needs and to liaise with teaching staff.

Supports can include assistive technology, library support and academic support. Contact the institution's disability office or access office at the beginning of the year. Please note that it is important to fill out the 'Med Box' on page 1 of the CAO form to avail of these supports.

Financial Supports/Scholarships

A fund is available for students with disabilities, which aims to facilitate study from Post Leaving Cert course level up to doctorate level. Contact the institution or its access/disability officer; they can make an application for the student following an assessment of needs. See also www.studentfinance.ie and click 'fund students with disabilities' for further information.

NUI colleges offer awards to first-year undergraduate students to the value of €11,000. See www.nui.ie for further information.

DCU runs a scholarship scheme for disabled students who want to combine their academic and sporting interests. For more information see www.dcu.ie/studentsport/scholarships.shtml.

As a parent of a teenager with a disability it is good to plan ahead of time in order to make the best choice for your teen and to ensure that they get the best supports and the best learning environment for them.

Appendix 5

Apprenticeships

College or university is not the best choice for everyone. Apprenticeships provide an effective route to careers and employers that require a trade, e.g. the ESB, Bord na Móna, the Irish Army, the Office of Public Works (OPW), hairdressing, etc. Apprenticeships suit the learning style and add to the confidence of the more practical teenager who likes to learn by moving and doing. Journalist Eoghan Harris says in praise of apprenticeships of that it is '[f]ar better to give these young people skills training instead of coercing them to do college courses, where they learn to become critics, rather than creators' (*Irish Independent*, 18 August 2013). Two main benefits of doing an apprenticeship are that they usually cost less than going to college and apprentices can earn money while learning their trade.

In Ireland, apprenticeships are controlled by Solas (formerly FÁS) in co-operation with the DES (see www.solas.ie).

Solas apprenticeships can be gained in the following trades and crafts, though there is a move to widen the range of trades on offer. (A person wishing to become an apprentice in one of the trades marked* must pass a colour vision test approved by Solas.)

- Agricultural mechanics
- Aircraft mechanics*
- Brick and stonelaying
- Carpentry and joinery
- Construction plant fitting*
- Electrical*

- Electrical instrumentation*
- Electronic security systems*
- Farriery
- Floor and wall tiling*
- Heavy vehicle mechanics*
- Industrial insulation
- Instrumentation*
- Mechanical automation and maintenance fitting*
- Metal fabrication
- Motor mechanics*
- Painting and decorating*
- Plastering
- Plumbing*
- Print media*
- Refrigeration and air conditioning*
- Sheet metalworking
- Toolmaking
- Vehicle body repairs*
- Wood manufacturing and finishing

Certain criteria must be met to become an apprentice. An applicant must be aged 16 plus and have a grade D in five Junior Cert subjects or equivalent; *or* be 18+ years old with three years' relevant work experience and pass an interview. Many employers advise applicants to have the Leaving Cert as many apprenticeships involve a high level of maths and science. Then the would-be apprentice needs to find an employer seeking an apprentice or willing to take someone on in order to master a trade. These employers must register with the National Training and Education Authority and must be approved by Solas. An apprenticeship involves 'on-the-job' training and 'off-the-job' phases in an IT or college of further education. There are seven stages of on- and off-the-job training, leading to an award at QQI level 6. The employer meets the on-the-job training costs and provides a wage, while the state bears the costs of 40 weeks' off-the-job (college) training and provides a wage for that period.

Among the highlights of the apprenticeship calendar each year are the National Skills Competitions. Normally, Dublin Institute of Technology hosts twelve finals annually for different skill specialisations on behalf of the DES and the candidates are likely to include representatives from other centres as well as from DIT. The overall winner in each trade area receives a silver medal from the DES and is eligible for consideration for selection for the national team, which represents Ireland in the International World Skills Competition (www.dit.ie/study/apprenticeships).

Apprenticeships are also available in the craft industry. It is possible to specialise in metal (jewellery making, silversmithing, farriering, blacksmithing), glass, clay (ceramics, pottery), textiles (textile artist, textile design) and wood (wood turning, furniture design). Refer to the Design and Crafts Council Ireland (www.dccoi.ie) and the Department of Education and Skills (www.education.ie) for more information.

Look under 'Apprenticeships' in the list of websites under 'Further Resources' for some employers that offer apprenticeships.

Appendix 6

Other Opportunities

Sometimes, for a range of reasons, we do not achieve our potential at school. We might not get the points we want or even know what to do when we leave school. However, there are many avenues that can take us in the direction of the career or qualifications we want. It just might take a little more time.

Foundation/Access Courses

Access courses are for students who for social, economic or educational reasons did not achieve their potential or are unable to access third level. Foundation or access programmes allow students to sample various subjects, gain confidence in academic learning and clarify their career or learning specialisms. They are a 'back door' into many programmes in higher education.

School-leavers can decide to take the Higher Education Access Route (HEAR). This is for students with the Irish Leaving Certificate and who are under 23 years old. HEAR helps applicants from disadvantaged socio-economic backgrounds to access college with lower points and to receive supports from undergraduate level through to postgraduate level. HEAR applicants must meet a range of financial, social and cultural indicators in order to be considered for reduced points places and extra supports. See www.accesscollege.ie for further information.

Some colleges run their own access programmes, for example the Trinity Access Programme (TAP) run by Trinity College, Dublin. Applicants must meet the HEAR requirements, but Trinity has its own application procedure. Contact the access offices of universities and ITs for further information on similar access programmes.

Post Leaving Cert Courses (PLCs)

PLCs (see also page 191) teach vocational and technical skills that can lead to employment or act as a stepping stone to higher education. They generally last one year and cover a wide range of subjects, including art, performance, equestrian studies, beauty, childcare, sport and leisure, catering and horticulture, etc. A database of courses is available at www.qualifax.ie. PLCs can offer a good qualification in practical skills and provide time for a maturing process before deciding on other options.

Mature Students

If you are 23 or older by 1 January in the year of application to CAO, you are considered a mature student. Mature students are assessed under different criteria from those that apply to school leavers. See www.cao.ie for further information. Aontas, the National Adult Learning Organisation, also provides information for mature students: see www.aontas.com.

Gap Year

Some young people take a year out to volunteer or do an internship overseas. Projects can involve work and activities in teaching, care, conservation and the environment, medicine, community and sports. Destinations range from Africa to Asia, Eastern Europe, Latin America and the South Pacific. See www.projects-abroad.ie for further information. Ireland's youth website, www.spunout.ie, also offers tips for a gap year and travelling in general.

Further Resources

Useful Websites

Knowing Yourself

www.assessment.com – online MAPP self-assessment of what motivates you
www.businessballs.com/howardgardnermultipleintelligences.htm – free tests
  on multiple intelligences and learning styles (VAK – visual, auditory and
  kinaesthetic)
www.careersportal.ie – Irish interactive careers programme
www.keirsey.com – personality assessment
www.myfuture.edu.au – Australia's career information and exploration tool
www.prospects.ac.uk – the UK's official graduate careers website
www.vark-learn.com – free online VARK questionnaire to find out what your
  learning style is
www.windmillsonline.co.uk – good exercises and advice

Occupational Information

www.candeguidance.com/subject.pdf – subject choice for the Leaving Cert
http://careers.nuim.ie – NUI Maynooth virtual careers library
www.dccoi.ie – Design and Crafts Council Ireland
http://gradireland.com/careers-advice/job-descriptions – comprehensive graduate
  information and graduate routes into areas such as teaching
www.insidecareers.co.uk – careers resource for the professions
www.prospects.ac.uk – see 'Jobs and work' and 'Explore types of jobs' sections
www.qualifax.ie – careers information

Disability/Access

www.accesscollege.ie/dare – Disability Access Route to Education (DARE)
www.accesscollege.ie/hear – Higher Education Access Route (HEAR)
www.ahead.ie – Association for Higher Education Access & Disability
  (AHEAD)
www.disability.ie – information portal site for the disabled community

Study and Finance

www.cao.ie – Central Application Office for undergraduate courses in Irish
  higher education institutions
www.citizensinformation.ie – general advice and information on public services
  and entitlements
www.studentfinance.ie – information on finance and supports
www.susi.ie – Student Universal Support Ireland (SUSI); student grant scheme
www.ucas.com – UK University and College Application System

FURTHER RESOURCES

Apprenticeships

www.careersportal.ie – often lists apprenticeship openings with the Office of
Public Works (OPW) and Bord na Móna

www.dit.ie/study/apprenticeships – DIT has a major involvement in
apprenticeships

www.esb.ie – offers apprenticeships

www.indeed.com – searchable database that includes apprenticeships and
internships

www.military.ie – entry levels as cadet, recruit or apprentice

www.solas.ie – the new education and training authority in Ireland; provides an
overview of the apprenticeship programme

www.teagasc.ie – information on agriculture-related apprenticeships

Year Out/Volunteering

www.activelink.ie – volunteering information, training and opportunities

www.carmichaelcentre.ie – largest shared services centre for the community and
voluntary sector

www.comhlamh.org – specialising in overseas volunteering

www.csv.org.uk – UK-based volunteering organisation for 16–35-year-olds

www.idealist.org – a global volunteering resource

www.suas.ie – supporting education through volunteering

https://www.usit.ie/ – student travel and volunteering

www.volunteer.ie – support and resources on volunteering

www.volunteerabroad.com – comprehensive volunteering website

www.vso.ie – funded programmes for volunteering abroad

www.wwv.org.uk – volunteering opportunities worldwide

Entrepreneurship

www.enterprise.gov.ie – Department of Jobs, Enterprise and Innovation

https://www.localenterprise.ie/ – 'first-stop shop' for starting your own business

www.ibec.ie – provides training and development for business

www.ida.ie – attraction and development of foreign investment

www.isme.ie – Irish Small and Medium Enterprises Association

www.kompass.ie – company search engine

www.sfa.ie – Small Firms Association

Creativity

www.artscouncil.ie – development of the arts

www.artsmanagement.ie – management of the arts

www.cmc.ie – Contemporary Music Centre

www.creativecareers.ie – information on creative careers

www.dancetheatreireland.com – professional dance company

www.iftn.ie – Irish Film and Television Network

www.theatreforumireland.com – the 'voice of the performing arts'
www.visualartists.ie – representative body for professional visual artists
www.voluntaryarts.org – promotes participation in arts and crafts in the UK and Ireland
www.writerscentre.ie – promotes literature and writing; provides training

Further Supports

www.jigsaw.ie – free and confidential support for young people
www.spunout.ie – information for 16–25-year-olds on how to deal with life's challenges
www.youthinformation.ie – youth information centres, a key resource for young people

Bibliography and Further Reading

Books

Adler, Harry, *NLP: The New Art and Science of Getting What you Want* (Piatkus Books, 1997)

Beck, Martha, *Finding Your Own North Star: Claiming the Life You Were Meant to Live* (New York: Three Rivers Press, 2002)

Bolles, Richard Nelson, *What Color is Your Parachute?* (Berkeley, CA: Ten Speed Press, annual, first published 2011)

Campbell, Joseph, Betty Sue Flowers (ed.) and Bill Moyers, *The Power of Myth* (New York: Doubleday Dell, 1989)

Canfield, Jack, Mark Victor Hansen and Les Hewitt, *The Power of Focus* (London: Vermilion, 2001)

Covey, Stephen R., *The 7 Habits of Highly Effective People* (London: Franklin Covey, Simon & Schuster, 1985)

Csikszentmihalyi, Mihaly, *Flow: The Psychology of Optimal Experience* (London: Rider, 1992 and 2002)

de Mello, Anthony, *The Song of the Bird* (New York: Image Books, 1984)

Dyer, Wayne, *What Do You Really Want for Your Children?* (New York: Harper Collins, 2001)

Faber, Adele and Mazlish, Elaine, *How to Talk So Teens Will Listen and Listen So Teens Will Talk* (New York: Harper Collins, 2006)

Gaffney, Maureen, *Flourishing* (Dublin: Penguin Ireland, 2011)

Gardner, Howard, *Frames of Mind: The Theory of Multiple Intelligences* (New York: Basic Books, 1983)

Harpur, Andrée and Quirke, Mary, *Sorted! A Survival Guide for Parents of Students Making a Career Choice* (Blackhall, 2011)

HEA (Higher Education Authority) *A Study of Progression in Irish Higher Education* (Dublin, 2010), www.hea.ie/sites/default/files/study_of_progression_in_irish_higher_education_2010.pdf

Holland, John, *Self-Directed Search (SDS)* (Florida: PAR, www.parinc.com, 1994)

Jones, Graham and Moorhouse, Adrian, *Developing Mental Toughness: Gold Medal Strategies for Transforming Your Business Performance* (Oxford: Springhill, 2007)

Jones, Peter, *Tycoon* (London: Hodder, 2007)

Kavanagh, Patrick, 'Stony Grey Soil' in *Collected Poems* (Penguin Modern Classics Poetry, 2005)

Lees, John, *How to Get a Job You'll Love*, 10th edn (London: McGraw Hill, 2009)

Losier, Michael, *Law of Attraction* (London: Hodder, 2008)

Maltz, Maxwell, *Psycho-Cybernetics* (New York: Simon & Schuster, 1960/1969)

Mooney, Brian, *Start Your Career Journey Here!* (Edco, 2014)

Padinjarekara, Francis J., *A Dewdrop in the Ocean: Wisdom Stories for Turbulent Times* (Mumbai: Awareness Arc, 2009)

Palmer, Blaire, *The Recipe for Success: What Really Successful People Do and How You Can Do it Too* (London: A & C Black, 2009)

Ponder, Catherine, *The Dynamic Laws of Prosperity*, revised edn (California: DeVorss & Co., 1962)

Robinson, Ken, *The Element: How Finding Your Passion Changes Everything* (Penguin, 2009)

Super, Donald, *Super's Theory of Vocational Choice* (1954)

Swindoll, Charles, *Parenting: From Surviving to Thriving* (USA: Thomas Nelson, 2006)

Williams, Nick, *The Work We Were Born To Do: Find the Work You Love, Love the Work You Do* (Element, 1999)

Williams, Nick, *Powerful Beyond Measure: An Inspiring Guide to Personal Freedom* (Bantam, 2002)

Wiseman, Richard, *59 Seconds: Think a Little, Change a Lot* (London: Macmillan, 2009)

Articles and Reports

Alberta Human Services, Canada, *Career Coaching Your Teens: A Guide for Parents*, http://alis.alberta.ca.//pdf/cshop/careercoach.pdf

American Psychological Association, *Resilience for Teens: Got Bounce?*, www.apa.org/helpcenter/bounce.aspx

Bates, Tony, 'Taking Control of Your Future', paper given at Trinity College, Dublin, June 2009

Bourke, Marie, 'Ireland's Future Skills Needs', paper given at the IBEC and IGC Annual Careers Conference, Future Expectations in Ireland's Evolving Economy, 23 November 2010

Byrne, Delma and Smyth, Emer, *Behind the Scenes? A Study of Parental Involvement in Post-Primary Education* (Dublin: ESRI, survey funded by NCCA and DES, 2011)

Donnelly, Katherine, 'Changes to CAO points system on the cards for 2017 exams' (*Irish Independent*, 27 April 2015)

GradIreland, *What Recruiters Want*, http://gradireland.com/careers-advice/cvs-and-applications/what-recruiters-want

Graduate Careers Ireland, *Focus for Success in Challenging Times* (Dublin: GCI, 2009)

Lee, Aileen, 'Scholarships: how to help your child land a scholarship' (*Irish Examiner*, 6 February 2015)

Murray, Niall, 'Males linked to growing drop out rate at third level' (*Irish Examiner*, 14 July 2014)

NLP Training, Training Notes, www.nlptraininginstitute.com

Sanders, Matt, 'Don't blame the parents, help them' (*Irish Times*, 7 June 2011)

Trinity College, Dublin, Transferable Skills Project 2006, https://www.tcd.ie/Careers/academics/collaborate/transferable_skills_project.php

Understanding Teenagers: The Blog, *10 Ways to Develop Resilience in Teenagers*, http://understandingteenagers.com.au/blog/2010/07/10-ways-to-develop-resilience-in-teenagers/

Walshe, John, 'Employers say graduates can't write well enough', quoting gradireland.com's 2010 survey (*Irish Independent*, 11 October 2010, www.gradireland.com)

Wayman, Sheila, '"We'll fix it": Parents do their children no favours' (*Irish Times*, 16 February 2015)

Young Minds, *Wellbeing*, www.youngminds.org.uk/training_services/young_minds_in_schools/wellbeing